# Promising Practices in

# CHARACTER EDUCATION

## VOLUME II

### MORE SUCCESS STORIES FROM AROUND THE COUNTRY

Introduction by Dr. Philip Fitch Vincent
Edited by Ginny Turner

Promising Practices in
# CHARACTER EDUCATION
Volume II

12 MORE SUCCESS STORIES
FROM AROUND THE COUNTRY

Introduction by Dr. Philip Fitch Vincent
Edited by Ginny Turner & Philip Vincent

Produced and published by
CHARACTER DEVELOPMENT GROUP

PROMISING PRACTICES IN CHARACTER EDUCATION, VOLUME II.
Copyright ©1999, 2004. Second Printing, Character
Development Group. All rights reserved. Printed in the
United States of America. No part of this book may be
used or reproduced in any manner whatsoever without
written permission except in the case of brief quotations
embodied in critical articles or reviews. For information,
address Character Development Group, PO Box 9211,
Chapel Hill, NC 27515-9211.
(919) 967–2110, fax (919) 967–2139
E-mail: respect96@aol.com
www.CharacterEducation.com

Cover design by Paul Turley
Book design by Janice Lewine
ISBN 1-892056-02-X

# ONTENTS

# ▓ Dedication

This book is dedicated to Pam Shelden, the late Director of Comprehensive Planning for Escambia County School District in Pensacola, Florida. As illustrated in Chapter 4, which she wrote before her death in 1998, Pam was deeply committed to the importance of character education in the life of the school and the community. The memory of her passion and work in this field continues to inspire all of us who believe that character and academics together reflect the true goal of education.

Thank you for a life well lived.

# INTRODUCTION

**Dr. Philip Fitch Vincent**

When Character Development Group published *Promising Practices in Character Education: Nine Success Stories From Around the Country* in 1996, we were venturing into a relatively new area. Much attention over recent years had been given to various approaches to address the affective education of children. Initiatives such as conflict resolution or service learning gained in popularity, but character education was suspect in some education circles as just a rehash of the controversial values clarification. The positive results seen in a variety schools across the country have shown it clearly was not. There is staying power to this movement. Led by the intellectual force of academics such as Kevin Ryan and Thomas Lickona, it has been energized by the enthusiastic response of educators and parents to dramatic improvements they saw in class climate and test scores.

It's ironic that character education is not a new concept. As Kevin Ryan has expressed, character education represents the oldest mission of America's schools and we're only rediscovering it. The first public schools founded in Massachusetts stressed how important it was to help children gain a strong moral underpinning. When they learned to read, they read the Bible and discussed resolution of moral issues. Children were taught to value a moral core and responsibility to their community.

When our nation was established, our founding fathers felt that a strong democracy called for an educated citizenry. They separated religious teaching from public schools, but retained as an essential part of education instilling civic and personal virtues that would benefit the family, the community, and our emerging nation.

This focus on moral and character education continued and evolved in schools as a crucial focus through the 1950s. I will not go into specifics in this piece to note how and why character education began a serious decline in the 1960s, but it's clear to me and many other educators and parents that a return to some kind of character education in the schools is an increasingly pressing issue as we enter the new millennium.

We are a little worried. Current statistics show that violent crime is decreasing among adults in America. Yet something is wrong that we see in our communities and schools. There seems to be less respect for teachers, community leaders, and others in authority, less of the basic civilities and courtesies between individuals—both of which are vital for a caring community and, ultimately, a thriving nation.

There are also concerns about an increase in juvenile violence nationwide. North Carolina, my home state, released a report on the increase of juvenile crime from 1987 to 1996. Violent crimes by juveniles were up 172%. Weapon law violations were up 482%. Drug violations were up 523%. All arrests for juveniles were up 105%.[1] In 1998, a report was released by the Educational Testing Service compared the percentage of public school principals reporting various discipline issues as being of serious or moderate problems in their high schools in the school years 1990-1991 and 1996-1997. The researcher noted that "there were several significant differences between 1991 and 1997. In 1997, more principals reported that student tardiness, absenteeism, class-cutting, drug use, sale of drugs on school grounds, and verbal abuse of teachers were serious or moderate problems."[2]

A report issued for *Who's Who Among America's Teachers* in 1997, noted that 81% of the veteran teachers (defined as teaching 10 or more years) felt that students were less respectful of authority and 73% were less ethical/moral.[3] We could go on and on about community concerns and school woes. We all know about the problem. The question for us, as educators, is What we can do about this within the school day? Our aim must be to create a civil climate in the school so positive character can be nurtured and developed. How might we begin our task?

First, we must acknowledge that we are not born knowing what the right or just action is. Children—as well as adults—must be taught through modeling, discussions, and direct instruction. Based on this premise, we cannot blame the kids. If they are acting in an inappropriate manner, we must accept the responsibility and began teaching them what is the correct way to act. Dr. William Damon, in his work, *Greater Expectations* (1995) notes:

> The seeds of the moral sense are sown at conception and its roots are firmly established at birth. Every infant enters this world prepared to respond socially, and in a moral manner, to others. Every child has the capacity to acquire moral character. The necessary emotional response systems, budding cognitive awareness, and personal dispositions are there from the start. Although, unfortunately, not every child grows into a responsible and caring person, the potential to do so is native to every member of the species (p.132)

The wiring is there to help children become good people. As adults we must provide the current and the oversight to make sure the system is not short-circuited by bad examples. In my travels, I've rarely met an individual who doesn't believe adults are the chief character developers of children. Children learn what they see, both good and bad. What we as educators must determine is how we impact on the character development of our students. Perhaps we should return to the ideas of Aristotle. In the *Nicomachean Ethics*, Aristotle notes:

> Excellence or virtue, then, being of two kinds, intellectual and moral, intellectual excellence owes its birth and growth mainly to teaching, and so requires time and experience, while moral excellence is the result of habit or custom (*ethike*), and has accordingly received in our language [Greek] a name formed by a slight change from the word ethos [meaning habit]. From this it is plain that none of the moral excellencies or virtues is implanted in us by nature; for that which is by nature implanted within us cannot be altered by training.... The virtues, then, come neither by nature nor contrary to nature, but nature gives us the capacity for acquiring them, and this is developed by training.

Aristotle provides us with what we need. First he separates for us two kinds of virtue. The first is intellectual, which develops over time and ideally involves a lifetime of experience, study, and reflection. Schools facilitate this process through literature and narratives. Simply reading great ideas or the Great Books is not enough: one must reflect on or discuss the piece to gain a greater intellectual understanding of the issues.

The second thrust of Aristotle's argument is the development of moral virtue, or the habits one needs to be a person of character. This is not teaching religion. This is common sense. We all want our children to learn to think well, to listen to the ideas of others—to separate sound reasoning and thought from that of charlatans. This is a part of what schooling should do for all children. To omit it leaves our mission half completed. We must also help children develop the character traits that will sustain them through life and make them the kind of adults we want to be leaders and participants in communities where we live. The school's mission must therefore be intellectual and moral in its aims. Anything less represents the miseducation of children.

Some observers consider this to be an impossible task. Can members of a community agree on the traits we deem essential for children to possess? Yes, they can. People all over the United States are taking the time to thoughtfully consider the issue of what children should learn in school. This exercise reflects a "coming together" of communities, as is clearly shown in the following stories. It's important to note that each community worked it out in its own way. This is not a weakness but rather a strength.

**Escambia County School District** began its efforts in reaction to a violent death of a young high school student on a school bus. Their efforts have had the support of the business community who are working with the schools to make Escambia County an ethical, values-based community.

**Calvert County Schools** in Maryland involved their community and all their schools in their efforts. Although excellence is seen throughout the county schools, the climate change found at the high schools is especially noteworthy, since at this level character education generally receives less emphasis than the "academics." Calvert County high school educators believe that academics and character go hand-in-hand.

Steve Dixon, principal of **Lilesville Elementary School** in Lilesville, N.C., explains how his total school focus on character education has resulted in a tremendous increase in his students' academic progress. He believes that as teacher modeling and student practices in civility increase teachers have more time to teach and students have more time to learn.

Gail Hartin, principal of **University Park Elementary School**, in Dallas, Texas, describes a five-year effort to improve the civil climate of her school. She emphasizes the importance of support from the school board and the superintendent.

The faculty and staff of **Atlantis Elementary School** in Cocoa, Florida, under the leadership of principal Vicki Mace, believe they must build a culture of respectful behavior, and model the practices they wish their students to learn. They emphasize inclusion, sharing and caring, encouragement of participation, and high expectations for every child.

Richard Parisi, principal of **Morgan Road Elementary** in Liverpool, N.Y., shares the experience of his school's extensive classroom, school, and community projects designed to foster the character development of their children. He has had tremendous support from his parents—94% of them agreed that character education in the school could positively assist them in their child's education.

Ivan Crissman, the principal of **Thomasville Primary School** in Thomasville, N.C., points out the importance of gaining school-wide consistency in the rules and procedures they designed to promote civility. He also notes a substantial increase in the measured achievement of his third graders (the only tested group in the school) compared to previous years. He does not attribute all the academic growth to the character education efforts, but acknowledges that the positive climate allows for innovative ideas to grow and develop.

Lynn Lisy-Macan, principal of **Brookside Elementary School** in Binghamton, N.Y., began by inviting parents, teachers, staff, and community members to a daylong meeting to discuss concerns about the school and children's education. A widespread concern of the parents centered on the lack of responsibility and motivation in their children. This helped launch their character-building efforts, which have experienced a great deal of support throughout the school building and community.

**Winston-Salem-Forsyth County Schools** in North Carolina have two schools featured in the work although it could have had many more. Rural Hall Elementary and Vienna Elementary schools describe clear examples of how character development must reflect the ethos or life of the school. Everyone is involved in the effort and as you will see, great things are occurring.

Finally, two teachers—Deb Brown, an elementary teacher from Charleston, W.V., and Charlie Abourjilie (formerly a high school teacher from Guilford County Schools in Greensboro, N.C., but now Director of Character Education in Guilford County Schools)—describe their classrooms and how they infused character into all their teaching.

What can we learn from these school districts, schools, principals, counselors, classroom teachers, and communities? First, we should walk away knowing that character education is not only doable, it can be done well. Second, we can learn that parents are supportive of well-designed processes that treat character not as an add-on program, but as part of the "ethos" or life of the school. Finally, there is a passion in each of these efforts. People believe strongly in what they are doing, and it propels them into taking character education as far as they can. Many have been through "this year's program" in their schools, and have had enough of fads. Character education reflects a life's focus. It's more permanent and much more important.

I trust you'll enjoy these stories of how character is returning to the schools in wonderful and innovative ways. I, for one, am honored to work with individuals such as the contributors to this book, and many, many others throughout the country. I am humbled by your dedication and deeply grateful for what you are doing to improve the world we all live in. God bless you all.

[1] Report released in by the state of North Carolina on Juvenile Crime 1986-1996. Cited in the *Charlotte Observer*, September 13, 1997.

[2] Ibid.

[3] Educational Communications for *Who's Who Among America's Teachers*. It appeared in graph form in *USA Today*, September 9, 1997.

# Character Education Permeates Every Aspect of School Culture

**Vicki Mace**

Principal, Atlantis Elementary School

Atlantis Elementary, a 722-student school in Cocoa, Florida, has been described as a school that sounds happy! The laughter of friendships, the absence of shouting, the greetings from all, and the character-building music reflect this caring community. It's common to see students greeting others and holding the door open for teachers as they enter their classrooms. Teachers interface with students and colleagues, and children greet the principal, Vicki Mace, with one of the "Three Hs"—hug, handshake, or high five. Kindergarten students give her a "thumbs up" greeting so they won't disrupt others' learning.

Dr. David Sawyer, Superintendent of Brevard Public Schools, proudly says, "Only a short visit to the school is necessary to observe the results of Atlantis' efforts. The students understand, appreciate, and model the character traits we all wish for our young people."

We at Atlantis Elementary School believe that we must build a culture and model the behavior that we want our students to learn. In addition, it is imperative we establish a positive climate which emphasizes inclusion, sharing and caring, encouragement of participation, and high expectations for each and every child. To create this safe, healthy, and caring environment, all the faculty and staff have dedicated renewed energies to implementing a character education program.

In 1995, Mrs. Mace, as the new principal, enthusiastically introduced character education. On the first day of preplanning, she shared with her staff her vision for building a community of learners. She initially implemented the LIFESKILLS program of Susan Kovalik (author of *Integrated Thematic Instruction: The Model* ), as the staff concentrated on building a positive school climate and promoting the importance of caring for children. After attending a two-day seminar with Dr. Philip Vincent the next spring and discovering material about the Character Counts Coalition, Mrs. Mace introduced the Six Pillars of Ethics: respect, responsibility, citizenship, fairness, caring, and trustworthiness. The staff felt that it was a "kid-friendly" approach and quickly agreed to make it our core program. Dr. Vincent's five components of character—rules and procedures, cooperative learning, teaching for thinking, quality literature, and service learning—became the guideline for a five-year plan of implementation.

Each month, one of the six pillars is highlighted for emphasis. To introduce it, Mrs. Mace presents the concept or the Character Counts Puppets may perform a vignette on closed circuit television. A daily Character Counts quote is given as well. The teachers receive the quotes in advance and one fifth grade teacher says that the quotes give an impetus for class discussion. In many classrooms the quotes are also incorporated as prompts for daily writing assignments.

In every classroom, including alternative education and day care, the six pillars are visible as a reminder of the words, concepts, and behaviors that are discussed in various contexts daily. Every bulletin board in the commons area portrays a message attesting to the importance of good manners and being a "kid for character." Large banners hang throughout the school to promote good attitudes and academic excellence. The Atlantis Code of Conduct—I am Respectful, Responsible, Trustworthy and Caring—is displayed in each classroom.

In recent years, we've seen many new ways to visually represent our character effort. In 1997, the art teacher created a school logo depicting our philosophy that we must educate the heart, hands, and the mind. Some teachers began to decorate their classroom windows with seasonal themes depicting the character traits. The concept of illustrating character quickly spread throughout the school and it's exciting to wander the halls each month to see how the different classes have chosen to illustrate character education. The art club students presented the school with a quilt that beautifully illustrates how character education is like piecing together patches of a quilt. The quilt hangs in the cafeteria for all to cherish. Triggered by a suggestion from a first-grader, we are in the process of painting the six words—respect, responsibility, fairness, citizenship, trustworthiness, and caring—on the columns which support the pavilion area.

In addition to finding the six words in various guises throughout the building, the students recite a pledge each morning prior to pledging allegiance to the flag.

Respect, Responsibility, and Citizenship, too.
They bring out the best in me and you.
Trustworthiness and being Fair
Help to show others that we really Care.
We all know what's right; we know what's good
We will do the things we know we should.

Each October an assembly is held to celebrate Character Education Week, and all parents are invited. In their testimonials, students cite learning the songs for the assembly as one of their favorite events. Every student, including pre-K and emotionally handicapped, participates in the schoolwide assembly and proudly wears a ribbon that states "Character Counts at Atlantis." Each grade level sings a song about one of the pillars. This year, Garry Smith entertained the audience with songs from his newly released CD "Songs in the Key of Character." It is very inspiring to see students, parents, and staff holding hands as they sing the song "We're Kids for Character."

Building a positive school climate is a significant component of our program. Each year a symbol and slogan are selected by the staff to serve as a common bond and reminder that children are our number-one priority in making decisions. This year's symbol is a smile, which can be found in every nook, cranny, and corner of the school. The symbols and slogans for the previous years include:

- 1996 - Star    *Together We Will Shine*
- 1997 - Heart    *Caring for Children is a Work of Heart*
- 1998 - World    *Building a Better World One Child at a Time*
- 1999 - Smile    *Every Child Smiles in the Same Language*

The schoolwide symbols have also been an effective means of integrating positive character traits into the curriculum. For example, it was natural to discuss respecting cultural differences and the environment when the world symbol was selected. The same lessons can be expanded this year as we look at children of different cultures.

## Character Is Not an Add-on

At Atlantis Elementary School, character education is not a separate course. It is a whole-school effort to create a virtuous community where behaviors linked to traits such as respect, responsibility, fairness, caring, trustworthiness, and citizenship are modeled, taught, and continually practiced in everyday interactions. Teachers now are quick to take advantage of opportunities presented in the curriculum to teach lessons about each of the six pillars. In addition, teachers make maximum use of teachable moments to create an awareness of the importance of good character.

The arts and extracurricular activities play an intricate role in character development. Through these courses of studies, qualities such as teamwork, persistence, responsibility, and cooperation can be learned. They also enhance students' connection to school, making them feel they are contributors to a vital community.

We have found that literature is a natural means of introducing the six core character traits to children. Good stories influence students' values and they can learn from the character's thoughts and actions. For example, students learn about differences among people in books like *Frederick and the Great Kapok Tree, Two Many Tamales* and *The Empty Pot* demonstrate that honesty is the best policy. The list of books to incorporate lessons of character is virtually endless. So are the many creative activities that can be developed from the reading series and classroom trade books, such as creating flip books that describe positive traits of the main character. Or having the class develop a checklist of characteristics that they feel describes a hero and measuring each character in the story to see if he meets the established criteria. A fourth grade teacher asked students to create license plates as a literature extension activity. She was deeply pleased to discover that the majority of the class drew plates that depicted messages for character education.

Incorporating character education into the writing program has been a rather simple endeavor. A few examples include writing in daily journals, creating class books about the character traits, and responding to daily quotes. Some teachers have students participate in writing activities to affirm positive character traits of classmates or to discuss why it's important to show you care for others. In preparing for the state writing exam, a fourth grade teacher created a lesson on similes. "A kid for character is like a bright sun in the sky," is one of the examples proudly displayed in the classroom.

Perhaps the most important first step in becoming a school which emphasizes respect, responsibility, and caring is the establishment of a positive school climate. According to Dr. Philip Vincent, "A good climate reflects high expectations of behavior and provides support for children to develop these behaviors." The discipline committee at Atlantis created a resource notebook that clearly states expectations for students, teachers, administrators, and parents. Specific guidelines for behavior in the classroom, hallway, on field trips, and during assemblies and dismissal, etc., are included. Guidelines for rules and procedures and assigning natural consequences were introduced and discussed at faculty meetings. Their purpose was to provide teachers with tools for classroom management and to create a good learning environment.

During the first weeks of school, the rules and procedures were discussed with students, and they were reinforced throughout the year. Expectations for student behavior are stated in the student handbook/calendar, which each student receives at registration. As a result of these efforts, a safe and orderly environment has evolved.

Mrs. Mace created a discipline form. Any student sent to the office with a referral must answer these four questions: *"Were you being a kid for character?"* *"Did you treat the other person(s) like you want to be treated?"* *"Did you stop and think?"* and *"Which pillar(s) do you think you need to work on to improve your behavior?"* The student must list three ways to demonstrate behavior that will reinforce the identified pillar. In conversation with Mrs. Mace, a plan of action is developed for the student if he finds himself in that situation again. She also developed additional activities to support each of the pillars if a child is repeatedly sent to the office.

## Positive Reinforcement Works

Every effort is made by administrators and teachers to catch kids "being good." We try to encourage students to demonstrate positive behavior without expecting an extrinsic reward. Mrs. Mace will thank students she sees walking in the hallway, greeting others, or exhibiting desirable behavior. She compliments the fourth and fifth grade students for being good role models and setting a positive example for the younger students. All classroom teachers serve as models, too, and often praise desired behavior when they see it.

In addition, Mrs. Mace tries to touch base daily with students who are exhibiting inappropriate behavior or academic problems to see what type of day they are having and if all work assignments have been completed. Some students, especially in the younger grades, respond better to receiving certificates and stickers, and we do use these to reinforce desired behavior. Teachers implement a variety of techniques to promote and recognize good behavior in the classroom.

Two schoolwide awards are presented weekly on the closed-circuit television to honor and encourage positive behavior. A student from each class who demonstrates responsibility, outstanding citizenship, confidence, kindness, enthusiasm, and trustworthiness, is selected by the teacher or classmates to receive a "ROCKET" award. A class from every grade level receives the "Best Bunch at Lunch" award for exhibiting the best behavior in the cafeteria.

Caring is the "glue" that holds our school together. Our conviction is that children don't care how much you know until they know how much you care. Teachers use daily classroom activities to create an environment that deems every member to be important, believes everyone has something to contribute, and acknowledges that everyone is someone special.

During the second week of February, Atlantis celebrates "Random Acts of Kindness Week." Each teacher receives a brochure describing activities and suggestions to encourage children to perform kind acts for others. The first year students received a "Kids Care Club" membership card for their kind deeds. In addition, they wrote their names on paper strips which were connected to form chains in their classrooms. At the end of the week, each classroom's chain was linked together to form one large chain to place around the cafeteria to celebrate the unselfish acts that were demonstrated daily. The following year, "Kindness Trees" were on display in the cafeteria and were decorated with heart-shaped ornaments on which children recorded their random acts of kindness. For the past two years, each classroom decorated a large heart to display in the cafeteria which illustrated the kind acts performed by the students.

We know that kindness is learned from those who give it. Our teachers serve as caregivers, mentors, and models for students. Each day, they create a caring environment in which students get to know each other, care about each other and feel valued as a member of the group. For example, Ms. Kledzik's fourth grade students call themselves the "Kledzik

Campers" and established a campers' code defining classroom expectations. A third grade class designed a T-shirt to enhance their classroom community. Others have created class banners such as "Helping Others + Kind Words = Mrs. Camp's Class." Many teachers incorporate class meetings to engage students in shared decision making and to instill the desire to make the classroom the best it can be. The meetings are valuable tools that provide an ongoing forum where students' thoughts are valued and where needs of the group can be addressed.

Another key goal is to help children develop a strong, positive emotional connection to school. Atlantis incorporates such activities as school traditions, student council spirit activities, schoolwide service community projects, and other activities in which students can shape and thus share ownership of school and class goals. Fostering a child's attachment to his school increases the desire and willingness to live by its values.

The Student Council, comprised of representatives from the fourth and fifth grade classes, is very active in promoting school spirit and coordinating schoolwide events to help build a positive moral culture. In December, Student Council encourages students to dress in the holiday colors and to wear various accessories such as necklaces, pins, socks, etc., to exhibit their school spirit. Some other activities sponsored by the Student Council include Crazy Socks Day, Twins Day, Favorite Cartoon T-shirt Day, Favorite Sports T-shirt Day and many more. Student Council also sells grams at Valentines Day and Christmas so students can send special messages to teachers and friends.

Atlantis has implemented school traditions the last four years that we hope give students fond memories of their elementary education. Each Friday, students are encouraged to wear their school T-shirt for school spirit. Prior to the Thanksgiving holiday, students and teachers have fun dressing as a pilgrim, pioneer, or Indian as they feast together outside. Each year, some of the braver and more physically fit faculty members challenge the fifth grade PE club to a softball match.

## Service Learning is a Critical Component

Service learning is the most rewarding component of our character education program. Doing kind acts develops "habits of the heart" and fosters an ethic of service and volunteerism. Service learning was never mandated, but it evolved as the students and staff became more aware of the needs of others. It is touching to see fifth grade students decide to give

Christmas gifts to needy families in the neighborhood instead of participating in the ritual of exchanging gifts with classmates. Some of the service learning projects include:

### Schoolwide Projects
- Collecting canned food for the Student Council annual canned food drive
- Implementing a recycling project (4th grade and exceptional education)
- Protecting and learning about Sand Hill cranes that adopted Atlantis as their habitat
- Working with Publix, a local business partner, to purchase food and gifts for needy families in the community
- Collecting money for tornado victims in Central Florida
- Creating a Big Buddy Club to help students in wheelchairs
- Collecting money for Arnold Palmer Children's Hospital Pediatric Cardiac Wing (Special donation made in the name of an Atlantis teacher's baby)
- Making care baskets for sick/injured staff members and parent volunteers
- Collecting children's books for Salvation Army, Crisis Center, hospitals, and Sharing Center (Student Council)
- Collecting school supplies for Honduran students
- Hosting a grandparents reception
- Collecting school supplies for Honduran children (Student Council)
- Collecting money for Kosovar refugees (Student Council)

### Classroom Projects
- Participating in Reading Buddies (primary and intermediate tutoring program)
- Donating money, food, and supplies to local humane society
- Adopting a Port St. John family for Christmas (class raised funds with a bake sale)
- Making decorations for Meals on Wheels
- Adopting five total acres of rain forest in Costa Rica, Brazil, and Bolivia
- Donating student-published books to area hospital
- Donating toys to orphanages in Romania
- Giving toys to a needy family instead of exchanging Christmas gifts with classmates

- Making cards for residents of a retirement home
- Adopting two manatees
- Singing for Senior Citizenship Christmas Luncheon (Chorus)
- Making Christmas decorations for local Burger King
- Making a "Sharing & Caring" basket for custodian and family at Christmas
- Earning money to purchase and take care of plants for school
- Performing at Thanksgiving and Christmas events (Chorus)
- Participating in the St. Jude's Hospital Math-A-Thon
- Participating in Operation Christmas Child
- Adopting a whale
- Creating a butterfly garden (Environment Club)
- Becoming pen pals with senior citizens
- Participating in "Trucker Buddies"
- Adopting Oak Hammock Trail Wildlife Refuge (Earth Club will build bird houses for it)
- Sending Christmas cards to troops in Bosnia
- Making jack-o'-lanterns for nursing homes

For six consecutive months Atlantis has received the distinguished "School of the Month" Award from Keep Brevard Beautiful for its outstanding environmental projects at school and within the community. The environmental club meets twice a week after school to maintain a butterfly garden and compost pile that was constructed on the school campus. This year, the club adopted part of a local wildlife refuge as its yearlong project. The students have been learning from local experts about various birds that live in the refuge area. More important, they've been constructing birdhouses to be placed at the refuge in the near future.

All members of the Atlantis faculty believe that an effective character education program includes a meaningful and challenging academic curriculum that respects all learners and helps them to succeed. As Thomas Lickona says, "One of the most authentic ways to respect children is to respect the way they learn." The Atlantis faculty has carefully scrutinized the curriculum to determine how to create an educational environment in which every student can be successful. Many hours have been dedicated to aligning the reading curriculum to ensure that students are familiar with Florida's Sunshine State Standards. A computer lab with individualized instruction was implemented this year to serve second and third grade children who have been identified as being at risk. Selected students in first through third grades attend classes two mornings a week before school for special assistance in reading. Groups of students who need to be scholastically challenged attend a special class to learn about algebraic reasoning and critical thinking skills.

The PTO and community business partners have been very supportive in our adventure to implement a schoolwide program. To demonstrate their support, the PTO purchased a bumper sticker that says "Character Counts at Atlantis" for each student to display on the family vehicle. The community partners have provided student incentives, food for special award celebrations, and mentors to help students who need extra help academically.

Weekly newsletter articles provide parents with suggestions and activities that can be incorporated at home to enhance the character education program. We receive many positive comments from parents indicating they look forward to the weekly tidbits. In addition, Mrs. Mace provides the faculty with numerous articles in the weekly teacher newsletter to help teachers enhance their moral learning environment.

## The Result of Our Character Education Program

Based on formal and informal assessments, it is evident that character education has had a positive impact at Atlantis Elementary School. The conscientious efforts of the faculty and staff to implement the six pillars of character education has created an environment conducive for learning and an atmosphere which promotes ethical and moral behavior. The following indicators illustrate what the character education initiative has meant to the students, staff, and community.

- For the past two years, Atlantis parents have completed a district survey to measure the school climate. In all twenty categories, the percentage of "excellent" ratings improved from the previous year. Eighty-seven percent of the parents rated Atlantis as "good" or "exemplary" on the 1998 survey.
- A report recently distributed by the district office ranked Atlantis fifth out of seventy-eight schools for student attendance. This is a true indicator that the students enjoy coming to school.
- As students learn to care and develop positive character traits, they experience success both academically and socially. Atlantis continues to excel academically, scoring above the state median in writing, math, and reading for the last four years. In 1994, 33% of the fourth grade students obtained a score of 3 or above (scale 0-6) on the

mandated state writing assessment. Last year, the percentage of students scoring 3 or above was 81%.

- The promotion rate has improved from 98.3 % in 1994 to 99.4% in 1998. Also, the out-of-school-suspension rate decreased from 2.0% in 1994 to 0.3% in 1998.
- The number of referrals has decreased drastically in the past four years. In 1998, there were 180 referrals, an average of one referral a day, a pattern that continues this year.

One of the biggest affirmations that the character education program has made a positive difference is how our students serve their school, community, and nation. Each year, the number of service learning projects initiated by the students has increased. From making decorations for a local nursing home to raising money for a children's hospital, students are learning what it means to be productive members of the community. The following examples illustrate the compassion and care exhibited by the Atlantis' faculty and students.

One of our teachers is expecting a baby soon, and she learned in December that it has a defective heart chamber. So, to kick off this year's Random Acts of Kindness Week, donations were solicited to help build a new heart wing at Arnold Palmer Hospital. A check for $1,200 will be presented to the hospital in the name of the teacher's unborn child and other children in need of special care. You never know how an act of kindness such as the "Give From the Heart for Baby Niemi" project may affect an individual. A mother of a first grade student stopped Mrs. Mace in the hallway during dismissal time to share a story about her daughter. Angelica received a nickel from the tooth fairy the previous evening. Instead of putting it in a special piggy bank to save for a special purchase, she insisted on taking the nickel to school for Baby Niemi. The mother shared her gratitude for creating such a caring environment and was quite moved by her daughter's generosity. Two other students donated $6.00 each that they received from their grandparents for Valentine's Day. Such unselfish acts of kindness are demonstrated daily by students. [Note: When the baby was born, the students were glad to learn his defect was not as extensive as his parents had been informed.]

You know that students are starting to understand the importance of "doing the good" when you witness a little boy whispering to Mrs. Mace during a teacher's observation that giving a piece of paper to another student is demonstrating citizenship. Recently, two young girls reported fifth grade boys who kicked the wall as they were leaving the campus because "they were not being respectful to our building." Or when a fourth grade student writes that he and his classmates always try to set an example for the little kids. The students hear the importance of being a good role model for younger students daily and it's rewarding to see them internalize the message and take pride in the important role they play in the school community.

The faculty and staff exhibit a caring attitude in all of their teaching endeavors. However, the following example demonstrates their commitment and dedication in helping mankind and serving as a positive role model for students. Mrs. Mace was contacted by an assistant principal from Rio Vista Elementary School in California about serving as a host school for two faculty members and two students who wanted to come to the area to view John Glenn's historic space shuttle mission. When the faculty received the request, two teachers graciously volunteered to open their homes for the visitors. In addition to providing lodging and meals, the teachers made special welcome baskets and hosted a party on the night of the launch in their honor.

Atlantis has included parents, business partners, and district resource personnel in its character education journey. Dr. Sally Shinn, Pre-K Resource Teacher, says, "I've seen a difference in how your school has embraced the very challenging task of educating severely handicapped students and the many complications that occur. I wish with all my heart that all students could be guaranteed the same approach and caring with common goals that appeal to virtually every religion and culture."

One parent commented, "The character education program at Atlantis has been a very positive experience throughout the school....I have seen it used in the classrooms as well as in the community....They learn not only what good character is, but what it looks like and how it feels." Another parent shares, "It is a comfort to know that the educators of my children will echo the teachings I have implemented at home....Although I will never be able to shield my children from the 'evils' of the world, I have peace of mind knowing that when they go to school each day, they are being instructed in the ways of kindness, compassion, and caring."

Probably the best way to see the result of our program to witness students applying values and ethical behavior in everyday interactions and discussions. As they become surrounded by teaching, practice, and modeling of ethical and moral choices, they internalize it in their decision making.

Four years after we started, we're still improving the program. The teachers have the opportunity several times a year to review the effectiveness of the program and comment on it. Mrs. Mace and several teachers have attended national conferences to become familiar with other successful programs. Research and new materials are discussed frequently with the character education committee and members of the staff. We are carefully examining Thomas Lickona's "Comprehensive Approach to Character Education" to see which areas need attention as we strive to improve the program.

In conclusion, character education is embedded in our school culture and integrated into the curriculum. It has become our vision and purpose in all decisions that we make affecting a child's education. As author Deb Austin Brown states, "The character lessons learned give our students a moral rope to hang on to in the decision times of childhood...and beyond." The Atlantis faculty and staff take the responsibility for creating a child's moral rope within his educational setting.

# $\mathscr{2}$ BINGHAMTON, NY

## Developing a Comprehensive Character Education Initiative: Brookside Elementary School's Journey

**Lynn Lisy-Macan**
Principal, Brookside Elementary School

## ❖ The Beginning

In the Spring of 1995, Brookside Elementary School in Binghamton, New York, was completing its first year with a new principal. We had had a shared-decision-making team composed of faculty from different grade levels, and we were getting limited participation from the teachers not involved in developing the annual initiatives. We decided to attempt a new format, and we were granted a day together to determine what our priorities were and what we would do to address the needs of our school community. We invited parents, teachers, staff and community members to our day-long meeting, and began by throwing out several questions, such as:

1. What do we like most about Brookside School?
2. What would we change if we could?
3. What have we thought about doing, but haven't gotten the chance?
4. What things would we like to try in the future?

Each group had teachers, staff and parents in it, and came up with answers to the questions. When we tallied the responses, we noticed a number of answers such as "I don't get the respect as a teacher the way I used to" or "Our kids are lacking in responsibility and motivation."

About that time, Dr. Tom Lickona was sponsoring the first Summer Institute in Character Education at The Center for the 4th & 5th R's: Respect & Responsibility, located in Cortland, New York. We decided to send a team from Brookside made up of the principal, a second grade teacher, and an intermediate special education teacher. Off we went, to the institute for five days of immersion in character education.ing Home

Although Dr. Lickona advocates for K-12 district initiatives in character education, the Brookside team was not prepared to be responsible for all five schools in our district (we are a district of 2,300 students, with three elementary schools, a junior high and a senior high). We first met with our Superintendent of Schools, and told him of our determination to start an intentional effort in character development at Brookside, and asked for his support and assistance. His response was that he believed we should begin on our own, and as soon as the other schools saw the successes that we experienced, they would soon follow.

We reviewed the materials we had received at Cortland, and discussed how best to begin teaching/sharing with the entire faculty. We did not want to have people return in September to mailboxes stuffed with information and run the risk of "turning them off" before we ever got started. We decided that the principal would do an introduction of some of the learning at the opening day faculty meeting, and that all faculty would be invited to join the Character Education steering group, which would first meet in the third week of September. We also felt it would be valuable to have an expert come to present the most crucial information to the staff, so we asked Dr. Lickona to do a half-day in-service for our entire faculty in October. We designated September through December as planning time, with a proposed kick-off in January 1996.

## Early Planning

A good representation of faculty and staff members committed to joining the steering group, and first decisions were made as to how our initiative would be structured. We faced many challenges, the foremost being how to involve all teachers while respecting their professional expertise and autonomy. The second was how to make our initiative comprehensive, so it touched all areas of our school community. We asked ourselves what we wanted the initiative to look like, what were our goals, and how would we know if and when we met them.

We had seen models of schools that had "word of the week," "word of the month," and configurations in between. After some discussion we agreed that we would focus on an attribute each month, which would be featured in the same month each year so our children would receive them as they were developmentally ready to.

The steering group developed a list of attributes they wanted to see included, but before we went further, we sent home a survey to parents. We acknowledged that parents are the first and foremost moral educators of their children, but said we wanted to work together on the task. We presented the proposed list of attributes and asked parents to contribute others. The response was encouraging and heartwarming: parents were interested in the same attributes we were, and not one parent responded negatively.

From there, we began planning, keeping in mind the five components that are important for comprehensive character initiatives:
- Be organized, systematic/ intentional
- Be literature-based and language-rich
- Be integrated—do NOT make character education an add-on
- Be sure to include all staff, parents and community
- Be visible in your efforts

## Our Attributes

These are the attributes we selected, and where we decided to place them within the school year:

| | |
|---|---|
| September: | Responsibility |
| October: | Respect |
| November: | Thankfulness |
| December: | Kindness |
| January: | Self-Control |
| February: | Tolerance |
| March: | Perseverance |
| April: | Friendship |
| May: | Honesty |
| June: | Cooperation |

*(See the end of the essay for how we define those terms)*

## Key Components of our Initiative

We knew that our teachers had more than enough to cover during the school year and we did not want to add more curriculum for them to fit into their day. Instead, we have encouraged our teachers to spend time reviewing their curriculum to find areas where they can integrate our selected attributes. Many found that Language Arts and Social Studies are the easiest places to integrate. Practically every novel has examples of character—both good and bad. Figures currently in politics, as well as those in history, represent all types of character traits. Now we are more intentional about highlighting those attributes.

All of our teachers are free to decide how to incorporate our attributes into their own classrooms, as well as how much time they spend doing so. Because the entire faculty committed to this initiative at the beginning, there's never a question whether everyone is participating. Teachers are comfortable because they're not asked to teach in a way that is stylistically or theoretically apart from their own beliefs.

Some of our teachers are setting goals for how many pieces of literature they cover each week related to the current attribute, and then have students writing literature response journals, keeping individual "character journals," and/or setting daily/weekly goals for how they will *exhibit* the current attribute.

Our expressive academic teachers (art, music, gym, library) are regularly incorporating the month's attribute into their curriculum, whether by creating student products that are displayed throughout the halls, in assemblies and at competitions, or by making references to the responsibility/respect necessary in use of materials, how we treat each other, and how we cooperate when in expressive academic classes.

Some teachers are creating performance tasks that incorporate our character education attributes while simultaneously meeting the New York State Learning Standards and the needs of differently abled learners.

Some are creating integrated math/science/technology projects that encourage students to reflect upon the various attributes that were necessary in completion of the task.

Some keep a separate bulletin board in their classrooms or in the hall near their doors, not only to highlight exemplary work that meets high expectations, but to exemplify the development of good character by showing how students have internalized the attributes.

How are our teachers able to accomplish all of that? One thing that contributes is release time for faculty. We have pursued grant funding and also received some district support for release time for our faculty to plan for curriculum integration. We began with a half day in the fall and a half day in the spring, when teachers could work independently or together by grade level to plan for their intentional character development within their curriculum.

Each year we try to provide more time. Many teachers are finding it easy to make these connections now, and don't feel that they need so much time to accomplish the integration.

## A Visual Culture

One essential element of our initiative is to develop and maintain a visual culture that communicates and reinforces our character expectations. We began by developing a logo (shown at the beginning of the chapter) which represents the affective, behavioral and cognitive domains in character development. Our motto is "Good character is...what you feel in your heart, what you think in your head, and what you do with your hands." It appears on our letterhead, is represented in our lobby, and soon will be on a flag flying with our American flag outdoors.

We maintain a large lobby display of our initiative. The first year we had just the words on banners; the second, we had the logo surrounded by the attributes on colorful strips; and the third, we made a bright, color-coded felt banner for each attribute, and our school mascot (a tiger cub) holds the banner of the month in his mouth as he greets students and visitors in the lobby.

Our Caring Calendar is developed monthly by students. It is another large lobby display with daily reminders about the attribute of the month. We have incorporated "Math Their Way" patterns into this calendar and the banners, as well as seasonal representations. Each day has suggestions on how to incorporate and demonstrate the month's attribute.

Periodically we develop a character-related theme  and have students develop hallway signs, posters and decorations. Recently we came up with "Good Character Hangs out at Brookside." Students cut out paper T-shirts, muscle shirts, shorts, socks, etc., and decorated them with pictures, poems, reminders and ideas about good character. We then hung "clothes lines" throughout the halls and attached the clothes with real clothespins.

Our cafeteria has large vinyl posters and banners, which are available from several companies now, and are daily reminders that good character is important everywhere—including the less structured environments of our school and community.

All of our buses have signs that tell students what the word of the month is, plus its definition and a reminder that good character is important on the bus!

We try to vary our visual reminders yearly in theme, and at least bimonthly throughout the school year. Part of this is accomplished through rejuvenation yearly at the Summer Institute.

## Ongoing Character Education Steering Group

Our steering group has two strands to it. Our teacher work day necessitates morning meetings from 8:00-8:45, when it's difficult for parents to attend because they're at work or have children at home. So we have evening meetings to accommodate them. The two meetings are on the same day, with the principal attending both, leaving us with two committees moving in the same direction, but meeting at different times.

The steering group generally meets once a month, though meetings are more frequent if there are assemblies and/or special decorating projects that need to be accomplished. These groups help immensely with the area of communication.

The parent steering group developed what we call the "Character Corner," which is published monthly in our local town newspaper, and sent home to parents with the "Caring Calendar" on the flip side. The Character Corner has a brief description of what our initiative's objective is with some suggestions for things that families can do together (some cost money, some do not) related to the character attribute of the month. We also provide a list of books, referenced by appropriate age, that families can read and discuss together.

We also created the "Character Minute." Our local ABC-TV affiliate comes to Brookside and films segments related to the attribute of the month. Sometimes they interview students, adults or parents, and sometimes they show a play, skit, song or assembly. The Minute is aired during the 6:00 evening news on Mondays. This has enabled us to keep our community informed regarding what we are doing in character education.

The Susquehanna Valley Central Schools elementary school lunch menu has a box at the top dedicated to character education, giving the attribute of the month and its definition. We know that the lunch menu consistently makes it onto the refrigerator and stays there! We regularly invite the media, as well as parents and community members, to come to our school and enjoy the assemblies, programs, and character education activities that we have.

# Whole School Gatherings

Another important element of our character education initiative is including opportunities for the whole school to come together for community building and sharing. In following the work of charater educator Chip Wood, who is co-creator of "The Responsive Classroom," we start out our school year with a "Welcome Back Day," for which the PTA decorates the school for the arrival of the students. The first hour of school is spent community building in individual classrooms, then the whole school comes together for an assembly. At the assembly, every adult in the school is introduced, we do some spirit cheers, and have a talk about friendship and good character. This is followed by lunch outdoors, a whole-school parade, and the whole school plays games together out on the fields just before going home. When students return after the year-end break, we do another whole-school assembly in January, including some goal-setting in character education and development.

Each month a grade level (one primary and one intermediate) is responsible for sharing the learning that has taken place related to the attribute. Sometimes grade levels plan assemblies that feature singing, skits, plays, poetry reading, literature sharing, etc. Other times, a bulletin board is created for the entire wing to enjoy, stories are shared, or games/activities are developed and shared throughout the building. The assemblies are important to remind children of appropriate behavior in large group gatherings, as well as because of the sharing that takes place.

Brookside has a Fine Arts Design Team that brings in artists in different media at least twice a year every year. We have found many authors, songwriters/singers and artists who are more than willing to integrate our character attributes into the presentations at Brookside.

Three times a year, Brookside has bus meetings, to discuss appropriate bus behavior. All of our students take buses, and we divide the groups from each bus into rooms throughout the school, and staff them with at least three adults and their bus driver. At the first meeting, we brainstorm what a safe and respectful bus ride looks like and sounds like, filling out charts that are kept for the later meetings. We do icebreaker activities to pair "bus buddies," who then sit together on the bus each day. The drivers talk about what rules they have on the bus, and why they are important. The second meeting takes place before the snow flies, to discuss safety issues related to winter weather, and the final meeting takes place in the spring, trying to head off the inevitable end-of-the-year slide!

Brookside's PTA has very much embraced the character education initiative. Together, we developed a "behavioral expectations" sign-off sheet that needs to be filled out and signed when children are going to participate in an after-school activity such a dance, karate, clubs, etc. The sign-off reminds children and parents what their responsibilities are, and that we expect good character from all who participate in after-school activities.

## PTA Partnership

Our PTA has sponsored "Turn Off the TV Nights," either once or twice monthly when they plan evening activities for parents and their children at the school. They encourage families to come to Brookside to enjoy a TV-free evening together. Some of the evenings have included Double Dutch jump roping, remote control car racing, family movies, bingo nights, pasta dinners, fashion shows, or entertainment nights. The PTA also sponsors an author who comes to our school each year to talk about her profession, and to read books to our students.

The PTA has established a mini-grant fund that enables our teachers to apply for money that might be difficult to find in the building budget for projects, trips and/or activities that they would like to do with their classes. The PTA meets and discusses the grants monthly, and so far has been able to fund just about every project that has been proposed—many of which have related to character education.

## Community Service Opportunities

Because our school is in a somewhat rural bedroom community, it's been difficult to facilitate community service within community settings (such as at nursing homes, hospitals, etc.), but we've been working on contributing to organizations that serve our community, as well as developing service learning opportunities (if the service is tied to curriculum, it's more likely to get transportation).

One winter when Northern New York and New England suffered the extreme ice storms and power failures, our school sponsored a food drive, and one of our staff members drove the collection directly to the north country, took pictures of the area and the agency that took our donations, and made a story board so the students could see how they made a direct impact on a community in need.

Buddy classes have worked together on projects such as collecting teddy bears for an organization that distributes them to sick children, food drives for specific community members in need, and collections for a nearby school that lost its playground to severe flooding.

Most recently, our own community had to pull together after we experienced several tornadoes on Memorial Day weekend. We had students/ families in our school who had completely lost their homes, and many more families who were without power for nearly a week and were also in need of food and a place to shower, etc. Other school families had massive property damage and needed assistance in cleaning up.

It was heartwarming to see both students and the PTA rally and organize to form a disaster relief fund that offered assistance to anyone in our town, whether they had children or not. It was a golden opportunity for students to put into action all that they have learned about good character. The donations were overwhelming—from cash to clothing and furniture. The most touching donations came from the children themselves, offering toys, books and items of their own so other children who had lost everything could have some fun returned to their lives.

## Keeping Our Initiative Fresh and Alive

Our character education initiative needs constant attention and daily commitment. Our goal is to have every staff member attend the Summer Institute in Character Education within five years. We find the Institute to be educational and enjoyable, as well as a source of renewal and rejuvenation for us. After attending the Institute, the steering group meets in the summer time to take stock and plan for the coming year.

We decide which elements of our initiative are most effective and should be continued (if in the same way, or in a different way), and which elements did not elicit the desired results and should be discontinued. Each year we try to have a new visual display in our lobby, as well as at least one new theme implemented. We try to provide between $1,000 and $2,000 to the school librarian for new literature linked directly to our character attributes, so that our initiative continues to be language-rich, and provides fresh material for our teachers to utilize.

Our school has been featured in two videos produced by National Professional Resources, Inc. One is "The Eleven Principles of Effective Character Education," the other is "Character Education: Application in the Classroom—Elementary." These videos are a great source of pride to our teachers, students and school district, and have been a networking resource for us. Schools from around the country contact us for information on our initiative, and we ask that they share what they do in their school.

Recently our school was selected to receive recognition from *Business Week* and the Character Education Partnership, and we were featured in the 1998 awards for instructional innovation *Schools of Character* publication, along with nine other schools across the country. This award not only provided recognition for our school and district, but supports us in our efforts to travel to other schools, conferences and institutes to share what has worked for us, and to help other schools to develop their initiatives in character education.

Our foundations are Dr. Thomas Lickona's twelve-point approach to comprehensive character education, along with the Character Education Partnership's "Eleven Principles of Effective Character Education." We have developed our own surveys for primary and intermediate students, and have implemented the survey designed to align to the Eleven Principles to assess the effectiveness of our efforts.

In addition, our teachers are provided with monthly reflection sheets that enable them to sum up "the best thing I did in character education this month"—be it a moment, a lesson, a unit, or a special activity or project. The teachers turn these reflection sheets in to the principal on a monthly basis, and the ideas are consolidated and shared so everyone can benefit from the creativity and energy of colleagues.

Parents have thanked us often for what we are doing. Many say, "I knew this was important, but didn't quite know how to tackle it, and the materials you send home have helped so much." Community members have recognized our efforts through phone calls, notes and comments. But what is most important, a change can be felt in our whole school community. We are intentional about first developing a caring community in each of our classrooms, and then carrying that over to a caring community throughout our entire school. Our students use the vocabulary and are internalizing the attributes.

Is our character education initiative the answer to every situation that arises in our school? For sure, the answer is "NO!" However, there is a heightened level of respect between students, students and teachers, teachers and parents, and even between staff members Brookside Elementary

School. Character Education has given our school a common goal. It's not just a program—it's who we are!

## BROOKSIDE ELEMENTARY CHARACTER EDUCATION CORE ATTRIBUTES

**Responsibility:** Responsible people are reliable, accept the consequences of their words and/or actions, can be trusted, take care of themselves as well as others, and are responsible for all they say and do.

**Respect:** To show consideration for the worth of self, others, living things, the environment, property and rules.

**Thankfulness:** Being grateful for the things we have, kindnesses shown, and the world around us.

**Kindness/Courtesy:** Being polite and helpful with our words and actions, and being thoughtful of how others feel.

**Self-Control:** Being aware of the thoughts, feelings and desires of others, then making a choice about how to behave.

**Tolerance/Acceptance:** Recognizing and respecting the opinions, practices or behaviors of others, even if they are different from our own, and welcoming new experiences and people into our lives.

**Perseverence:** Sticking with a task and not giving up, even when it's hard.

**Friendship:** A relationship between people who know, like, trust and support each other.

**Honesty:** Being truthful and fair to myself and others.

**Cooperation:** Being willing to be helpful and work together to achieve a common goal.

# $\mathscr{J}$CALVERT COUNTY, MD

## Transformation of School Climate Through a Character Development Program in Calvert County Schools

**Greg Miller**
Calvert County Schools

Calvert County school administrators, teachers, parents, and community are seeing a transformation of school climate through a state character education grant that integrates a character program with the existing curriculum. Practices that emphasize positive character and positive role models for children have led to an improvement in school climate measurement indicators, an increase in state performance assessment rankings, and an increase in more democratic ideas within the classroom.

Calvert County, with a population of 72,000 residents, is located between the Patuxent River and Chesapeake Bay, approximately forty miles from both Washington, D.C., and Baltimore, Maryland. The Calvert County Public Schools is a singular functioning county school system serving 14,000 students. We have have twenty-one schools: a special education center, a career center, eleven elementary schools, five middle schools,and three high schools. We are small enough to have a large-scale character education program implemented with little difficulty.

As a bedroom community for both Washington and Baltimore, and with recent military base expansion, Calvert County has had unprecedented growth in the last 15 years. This has proved a challenge in school construction and has changed our demographics. We have many new familes with children at both ends of the socioeconomic spectrum.

At the same time, our school board officials had been concerned with the lack of positive character traits exhibited by students. In conjunction with community officials and parents, the board adopted the school theme of "Discipline, Hard Work and Values" two years ago. Board members wanted to reflect the development of our students among a more traditional family values orientation, which our school parents indicate is an appropriate way to raise children. To promote the theme, former assistant superintendent John O'Connell applied for and received a state grant to implement a character development program in the county.

## Getting Started

Calvert County's model for implementing the character development program uses an "action team" approach. This consists of a school improvement model with three branches to it—the instructional team, the school and community team, and the school climate team. Each teacher selects one of the three subcommittees to serve on during the school year. Character education falls in the school climate domain.

The group that works on character development activities within each school site serves as an ad hoc committee of the school improvement team. The action team at each site is responsible for developing school improvement goals, objectives, and activities in concert with the school's overall school improvement plan, while building a broadly based consensus among the entire staff. While character education is sometimes an add-on to the school improvement plan, our preferred approach has been to incorporate character education in as many strategies of the school improvement plan as possible. In short, the subcommittee responsible for character development reaches out to the other two parts of the umbrella.

Another important part of our model involves the use of a district steering committee, with a member from each of the twenty school improvement action teams, and supplemented with outside groups such as the Calvert Clergy Council, the County Chamber of Commerce, and the Business and Trade Commission. This committee provides ongoing advice and input for this district-wide, K-12 approach. Likewise, the steering committee members serve as liaison with the district and other school improvement teams.

Opportunities are given in each school for this to happen. Teachers share the minutes of each monthly meeting with their principals and at staff meetings. This sharing is critical—school administrators, both in the central office and in the school, must provide time for the liaison to disseminate information and obtain input from staff and community members. Time must be allowed to let the staff discuss what they might do and what they are already doing in their classrooms.

We have ten in-service days a year, with approximately five of those days reserved for in-house meetings. Each principal was urged to use some of that time to further the character development program in whatever way that principal chose. It was important that the administration give the character development program a focus in the schools, an effort that would show their support of the program. To be effective, support for the character development program must cross all lines.

## Gaining Consensus: The Great Eight Character Traits

After grant approval, county officials set out to structure the program to get it started in the 1996-97 school year. The goal the first year was to have a smooth transition into this program, with a planning and training effort to begin that summer, followed by more effective ways to implement the program. The action team approach, akin to quality circles, kept the program focused and moving forward.

One of the first tasks was to decide how this character development program would best fit into our existing curriculum. A steering committee that included administrators, central office staff, guidance counselors, teachers and community leaders provided the initial impetus for a district-wide and community-wide effort. The focus of this first group was to establish consensus on what character traits to emphasize. The group decided to highlight a character trait for each month, or in some cases, months. The group identified and defined the following traits:

**Respect** (August/September)—To show consideration for the worth of self, others, living things, the environment, property, and rules through my words and actions.

**Responsibility** (October)—Able to be trusted or depended upon to carry out duties in a timely way.

**Caring** (November/December)—Concern for well-being of others.

**Justice and Fairness** (January)—Treating people honestly and justly, respecting the roles of society and the rights of others.
**Honesty and Trustworthiness** (February)—Being truthful and trustworthy.
**Self-Discipline** (March)—Applying ourselves to our tasks and being able to delay gratification in order to develop your talents and work toward distant goals.
**Integrity** (April)—Being faithful to good principles and high ideals.
**Cooperation** (May)—When two or more people work together by combining their talents and abilities to reach a common goal.

Some traits seem to fit well with particular months. For example, caring encompasses Thanksgiving and Christmas, while honesty is often associated with presidents Lincoln and Washington. Students work in groups on a state assessment in May, so cooperation became a logical choice for that month. Group members realized there are many other traits, and that character cannot be defined by how well you exhibit each particular trait; however, they chose these traits to launch the program. There appears to be overwhelming consensus concerning the establishment of what Dr. O'Connell labeled as the "Great Eight Character Traits."

## Getting Started

After gaining consensus on the eight character traits, school officials decided that the implementation of the program rested with their faculty. As one career center teacher said, "People will work for you on this if you don't tell them exactly what to do." Teachers address the program in different ways. Each is allowed to promote and discuss character in his or her own way, though we provide a framework teachers and administrators can work from. We also had to provide easy, efficient ways of getting teachers started with activities that integrate character development.

There were several reasons for this. The Maryland State Performance Assessment Program has been a big thrust in our county for the last seven years. Whole curricula have been revamped to focus on more performance-based instruction. National standards are also driving some curriculum changes. Three years ago our district implemented the Core Knowledge Curriculum in grades K-6, and developed an essential curriculum for the high school. High school student also take course exit exams at the end of each school year.

Character development planners understood there have been many changes and add-on programs to an already large and difficult curriculum. Many schools were doing something already for character development. Many of our selected character traits were already a large part of our school settings and curriculum, especially those dealing with respect and responsibility.

In some places, like at St. Leonard and Appeal Elementary, the "Three Rs"— respect, responsibility, and the right to learn—have been an integral part of the school's philosophy for a number of years. At Mt. Harmony the positive action program had been in place for several years. Program planners were challenged to make the character education program a structured and cohesive county-wide effort.

## Integrating with Existing Curriculum

We try to have character development pervade every aspect of the school and community life. Teachers across the county display the character traits on their walls or bulletin boards. Some wear a badge with the character trait of the month on it. Signs are put up around the school, usually by art students studying calligraphy. Many schools display the monthly character trait on their changeable outdoor sign. Students in many schools had a contest to pick a slogan that would go with character development. Patuxent High School uses the phrase "Don't just know it, show it."

Teachers have indicated that having the character traits posted gives them an easy way to discuss the character trait as they may come up in classroom teaching. For example, students may begin to take a test. Normally, a teacher might say, "Don't look at anyone else's paper" or "Don't talk during the test." The students themselves may not yet have internalized the character traits (such as self-discipline or cooperation) this situation calls for, and the signs let teachers bring them up. They may point to a sign and ask, "What does self-discipline mean in a test-taking situation?"

Schools have found many creative ways to sneak in character development ideas into almost every area of the school day. One involves putting the character trait and helpful suggestions on character development into the monthly lunch menu. These menus are posted in every classroom and the cafeteria; in the elementary school, these menus go home. Some cafeteria workers have given names to some of the menu items, such as "self-discipline spaghetti" or "caring corn."

Northern High School does a short segment each day about the character trait on its morning television program, which is shown to the entire student body. Some schools have mentioned the traits in their morning announcements. These are usually made by the school secretary, principal, or a guidance counselor. Other schools put the traits on a homework calendar that goes home with every student. One elementary school and one high school do a weekly homework folder, which has the character trait written on it.

In October, students at Southern Middle School read a poem about responsibility and then select a particular behavior they could do to practice that character trait. Students set a goal for the month, and use a picture of a thermometer to visually display their progress toward the goal. The goal was something that the students discussed and chose, and it could involve something other than schoolwork. Parents, of course, thought this activity was a great idea. Many of them reported seeing a positive change in students' behavior at home. Many students set goals every month of the year.

One idea that has proved useful at the high school is using student contracts and student feedback forms about character development issues. For example, teachers have found that an honest dialogue about what teachers and students want of each other is important. Students are asked to fill out this form at the beginning of the year as part of the attempt to create a positive atmosphere in the classroom. Teachers use it not only to get to know their students better, but also to start a discussion about how the classroom can be run more effectively.

High school students read some of the great literary classics, such as *Huckleberry Finn, A Separate Peace* or *Julius Caesar*. Discussions about these fictional characters can be used to think about character. Cathy Yeager wrote the word "respect" on the board, and then spent two weeks reading, discussing and doing activities on short stories she had selected that had something to do with respect. Then students completed a performance-based assessment that revolved around the respect theme. For responsibility, one high school teacher had his students discuss goal-setting and responsibility after reading Ben Franklin's autobiographical journal. Students then completed their own journal about improving their own lives.

Literature-based discussion on character can come as early as first and second grades. Kids relate to story and plot much more easily than explanatory forms that refer to character because children at an early age tell stories.

## Parent/Community Support

Parents were the easiest group to get to buy into having a character development model in the classroom. Parents got involved within the school in a number of ways. Parent volunteers put up the character traits signs around the school; one person prepares a glass case display each month that includes materials, saying, and pictures about that month's trait. Southern Middle School's Parent Teacher Student Association (PTSA) newspaper includes the word of the month, a published article about character development, and an article about students who were nominated for admirable behavior by their teacher. In some schools, the PTA has provided financial support for awards or other materials that might be needed. We let the community know about the program before it was implemented. In the summer before the first year, we invited the newspaper to write several articles about what the character development program was going to entail.

School personnel have asked local businesses to display a poster with the trait of the month and its definition on the sign. We've also gotten mentions on Sunday church bulletins. Usually these signs spark some conversation, such as, "What is this all about?" or "What are you doing in the schools?" A number of fire companies put on demonstrations and talks about fire safety in October. October has fire-prevention week, and responsibility is that month's character trait. At many schools, the idea of the fire company visiting is not new; however, now the fire department representative can refer to the character trait that is closely tied to fire prevention—namely, being responsible.

## Transformation of School Climate

In the short time since Calvert County Public Schools incorporated character development as the backdrop for all school activities, the school climate in many schools has been very positively transformed. One beneficial side effect has been the escalation of democratic principles in classroom use. In order for this program to work, students must see notions of respect and caring in everyday school situations. Teachers have been using more democratic means of working with students to foster this sense of respect and caring throughout the day.

The use of any kind of classroom meetings has increased in the past year, especially in the middle school. Many videos that show how to conduct class meetings that staff members may watch at home or see at a staff meeting. In addition, fifteen of our twenty-one schools now use some form of peer-mediated conflict resolution. They include all of our middle and high schools. In most of them, one trained teacher and/or guidance counselor coordinates the training of student mediators and coordinates the resolution meetings. This helps further discussion and concentration on character development issues.

Student government has taken on a new dimension. The emphasis for many school student councils has changed from a social organization to one that works in a collegial fashion with the school staff. Some schools are using the idea of a student advisory group or council to involve students in school governance. It is made up of delegates from each grade selected by teachers and/or classmates, and officers elected by the entire student body. Classroom delegates meet to draft rules for acceptable behavior and a list of consequences. The delegates go back to the classroom and get feedback on these rules. The delegate votes as his or her constituency wishes. The delegates can't take formal action on any issue without input from class meetings. This enables students to have practice in citizenship.

Guidance counselors Allyson Sigler at St. Leonard and Doug Verlich at Calvert Middle School each created a Character Traits Committee at their schools. Different students serve on the committee each month to coordinate activities in and around their classroom that emphasize that month's trait. Students have an "executive lunch" with Alison and Doug at the beginning of the month to plan the activities for the month and make posters to display around the school. These same students coordinate the "Leo-grams" and "Tiger-grams" messages to be read during morning announcements. These messages spotlight students who display that month's character trait. The committee has follow-up sessions during the month.

The students in these two schools are the focus of the character development movement. They are making the idea of positive character development their own. Children know that they can affect the quality of the school environment. Shared decision in collaboration with the adults in the schools makes this process an important building block in a young person's behavior.

Many schools have used the idea of student advisory or character committees to work on areas such as cafeteria, hallway and bus behavior. For example, teachers often had to be out in the hallways to move students along, keeping them from congregating and blocking traffic, keeping the noise down, and in the case of many of our crowded schools, making sure students keep one-way lanes. This monitoring added to the litany of staff duties during the school day.

However, in schools that discussed acceptable forms of behavior with student advisory groups, students conduct themselves in a more orderly fashion. They have come to realize the importance of making the school run safely and efficiently. At one school, a second lunch was created, the chips were moved over to the snack line, and all is better after students and staff members got together to solve a problem. Teachers are realizing that students can manage and improve their school environment. Students feel empowered by being allowed to offer their opinions and feelings in a number of areas regarding school governance, and this will help them want to work to build up a caring community. Teachers have to be role models within the building, parents have to be role models at home, but students also have to be role models for each other. The role of teachers shifted to working with students, not doing something to them.

This has even filtered down to our staff members' personal lives. Some of them indicate that relationships with their children and spouses have gotten better, because they think about how they themselves want to be treated, and act accordingly. A character development program that is focused and structured has transformative powers, both in the classroom and outside it.

## High School Transformation

The intention is not to isolate character development in a ten-minute curriculum add-on. Instead, we wanted to weave character into our everyday existence. The most successful attempts to better student character are at the elementary level. However, we found that high school students have a willingness to change their behavior and think about their character. Some of this was unplanned and quite surprising, given the pressures of teenagers today. Many teachers had assumed that the high school students would react most negatively to discussions about character. At all three high schools, students are collectively making the character development issue their own.

Students are Calvert High School got together and posed the idea that they would like to have their own honor code, much like colleges and military academies had. They wanted it, however, to be their own creation. Obviously, the staff was happy to have student involvement in their character development. This honor code went through the student advisory committee and was refined a number of times. The entire student body got to see this document.

The best example of how the character development program has worked is in Calvert County Public Schools' Career Center. Students from all three high schools may attend the career center for one half of the day. Staff at the career center know the work ethic and on-the-job behavior are intrinsically linked to character. They talked about all eight character traits and how they were important to getting and keeping a job. They were pleased to see the ideas were sinking in. The most noticeable difference was in the deportment of the students. Many referrals in previous years had stemmed from a student's refusal to wear clothing or uniforms appropriate to the profession they were learning. At the career center, students started wearing the appropriate uniforms, and the number of referrals for improper dress dropped 80 percent in one year.

Another area of concern was safety. Students at the career center were referred to the office for conducting their trade in an unsafe manner. Students themselves drafted a series of rules and expectations concerning behavior. The rules varied according to the profession; for example, a carpenter would have safety rules concerning use of equipment, working on roofs or ladders, while an electrician would have rules pertaining to electrical safety. Since the character development has been in place, the number of referrals for safety violations has decreased dramatically.

## Individual Classrooms

In individual classrooms, teachers have launched many successful projects, such as the self-discipline chart. Students complete a graph based on several statistics that indicate their behavior. It is called the counting-and-cheating activity and is used for students to keep track of times that they exhibit problem behavior. At the end of the week, students complete a graph, and by studying it, can start to analyze where and when they have the most problems. Teachers can set up goals along with each student to decrease the occasions of problem behavior.

Students naturally can find links between what they read and their own character. Often this internalization lends itself to reflective writing about character. Many teachers use journals in their reading and English classes. Teachers have used story starters that relate to character development, such as "A problem I'm having in school this year is..." and "I wish

I were able to...." Teachers can discuss character in written comments on students' papers. These comments not only relate to character, but they also show students that the teacher has read their comments and cares about them.

In Troy Sirman's science class at Calvert High, students discuss environmental issues and how respect relates to the environment. Students do experiments to show the effects of respecting and not respecting the environment. Some science teachers also discuss the ethics and integrity needed in this scientific community. For example, students read about the ethics involved during Einstein's era and the harnessing of atomic power, and reasons for sharing information in the scientific community.

## Evaluating the Results

The Calvert County Public Schools has in place a school climate survey as part of the school improvement plan. We have used this survey for a number of years. Certain parts of it, given to teachers near the end of every year, relate directly to school climate and character education. We also analyze discipline referrals, disciplinary actions and problems. Each school tracks the number of referrals each month and what character trait was not exhibited by that referral, using the year prior to the program implementation as baseline data. Referrals are down in many schools, and serious offenses are also down across the board. Student achievement concerns are also addressed on the effective schools survey. Character helps students achieve and gives them a protocol of behavior in the classroom and at home.

Some schools have used existing surveys to gain some impression of how the program is going. Some school climate chairpersons use a simple survey given out three times a year at staff meetings as the teachers are walking in. The survey takes only five minutes, but it provides some assessment and feedback on how teachers perceive the program is working. Monthly meetings provide an opportunity to share new ideas among school sites and informally evaluate the effectiveness of the program.

The school climate survey has indicated that there is an increase on the indicators that directly relate to character education. In fact, our entire school climate scores have increased in the last few years. The number of students in our Academically and Intellectually Able (AIA) class has increased in many of the elementary schools, and Calvert County's state ranking on the MSPAP assessment has increased to third place among twenty-three school districts. Early results indicate that there may be a possible link between the character education program and the improvement in student achievement seen in the county over the past two years.

There are other indicators of the program's effectiveness on the daily lives of everyone in the school building. This program has not only changed the perceptions of the school as measured by the survey, but it has affected even the teachers, administrators, and parents. For example, thinking about the character traits and what they mean has made the teachers and administrators think about their own behavior and how they interact with others.

## Conclusion

Children need the reinforcement of seeing all members of society acting in good and appropriate ways. Administrators, teachers, parents and community members must support character development programs and must model good character to show students that this is an acceptable and valued way of behaving. Teachers say they don't complain as much anymore or disparage any students in the faculty lounge because they know if they want their students to be respectful, they themselves should be.

Teachers say they use the ideas of democratic schools more in their classroom. Students are given an opportunity to talk about what is going on in the classroom, and how they feel about being in the classroom. Developing character has opened up for them new ways of seeing their responsibility to develop in students good behavioral practices that will last well into their future.

**References**

Lickona, Thomas. *Educating for Character: How Our Nation's Schools Can Teach Respect and Responsibility.* New York: Bantam Books, 1991.

# Escambia County School District Initiates a Core Values Program

**Pam Shelden**
Director, Comprehensive Planning

The death of a young high school student on a school bus was a call to action in the Escambia County School District in Pensacola, Florida. The incident came on top of an increasing level of violence in the community, a growing sense of community disintegration, and public dissatisfaction with the public schools. Because of all these factors, Superintendent Bill Maloy launched a dialogue about core values in our community. He had experienced the core values program in the U.S. Navy, and Dr. Maloy believed that a focus on "ethical expectations" was imperative for our schools.

The core values initiative in the Escambia County School District started in March 1993. Dr. Maloy announced to district employees that his plan to implement a set of core values would provide a framework for all district operations and reflect the kinds of ethical behaviors expected of all citizens. He called together parents, educators and representatives from local businesses, churches, the military and the Chamber of Commerce to serve as a task force to examine ways for reinstilling ethical behaviors and values into the school and the community.

Several meetings were held from May through July. In July, Dr. Maloy, along with senior school district administrators, entered into an agreement with CorVal, Inc., a consultation service from Clearwater, Florida, to facilitate the selection of core values and determine an implementation plan for the district.

In August, CorVal, Inc. distributed a values audit survey to selected employees to determine their perspectives of the district and its operation. Principals, district employees and school board members participated in the written survey and did personal interviews as well. In September, the superintendent, senior administrators, two principals and a school board member attended a retreat to draft core values for the organization.

During September and October, the group conducted interpersonal and subcommittee work to review and modify the initial draft of the core values statements. In October, a follow-up management retreat was held to provide an opportunity for a preliminary review of the survey data, to finalize work on the core values, and to determine an action plan for positive change in the Escambia County School District.

After extensive collaboration as part of a total quality leadership team-building initiative, Dr. Maloy and his management team agreed on a set of six core values: honesty, integrity, patriotism, equality, respect and responsibility. The core values were announced to the school district employees through an employee memorandum and to the public through a news release. A workshop for principals was held at which time they were encouraged to infuse the core values into their school operations. A Facilitators Manual was developed for use in school-based workshops.

Reaction to the core values was mixed. Some employees embraced the core values and appreciated the structure they offered for focusing on ethical expectations. Others questioned the authority of the management team to "insinuate that core values were not already being taught and modeled." Still others wondered why the schools were focusing on values; wasn't that the job of the parents or the religious institution?

## Core Values in Action Awareness Campaign

In February 1994, the next step was to take what was an abstract notion for some people and "bring core values to life." To head this initiative, the superintendent tapped Pam Shelden, director of comprehensive planning, who brought together a cross-section of stakeholders to create the Core Values Awareness Committee. The committee's goals were to develop ways that encouraged the district-level and school-based employees, as well as members of the community at large, to focus on core values. The committee addressed awareness, training, infusion into the curriculum, and development of a marketing plan.

A logo, slogan, and print materials for the district were designed. Posters, bumper stickers and  bulletin board headers were printed and distributed for use in school classrooms and hallways, district offices and buildings, and in prominent spots in the community. School "awareness packets" were developed with camera-ready art, bulletin board ideas and other school-based materials. A school survey was conducted  to find out what was already happening in the classrooms and again to heighten awareness of these activities. The ideas were compiled and distributed through a newsletter entitled "Core Values in Action!"

Many of the schools already had programs such as Social Skills and Stop and Think in place. The suggestion was to incorporate the six core values into these existing programs so a common vocabulary would begin to emerge. When children hear the words "respect" and "responsibility" at school and talk with their parents about what they have learned, mom and dad might have heard these same words in training at their own jobs.

## Training Efforts

In August 1994, selected principals were invited to become Principal Trainers for Core Values. An initial meeting was held with the principals to explain that their responsibilities would be to train other district personnel and to get involved in the community as trainers and speakers. Six principals agreed to go through training conducted by CorVal, Inc. and to fulfill their commitment to train others in the district and in the business community. The training effort was expanded to include personnel from the Pensacola Area Chamber of Commerce and Gulf Power Company. A cadre of trainers from the community soon was in place.

In September 1994, the six core values were included for the first time in the Student Rights and Responsibility Handbook, which was distributed to all 44,000 students in the district. Beginning in October, the Principal Trainers and district staff met to develop the training module which would be used in the school district. They decided that a series of workshops for principals and key school staff would begin the second semester. The premise was that the school "team" who attended the training would return to the school and conduct training for faculty, staff, students and school advisory council members.

Gulf Power Company, a major partner in education, joined in the training efforts. The workshop module was designed to include a presentation by one of the company's vice presidents to share the corporate perspective on core values.

The training modules included both large-group presentation and small-group interaction. Role-playing in scenarios that were real-life situations at school, home and the work site called upon people to make ethics-based decisions. The dialogue that followed was important to the process of internalizing the values and making them applicable to the individual.

In the meantime, the school district began a strategic planning process. A mission statement, vision statement, guiding principles and district goals were developed to incorporate the core values. Beginning in March 1995, a series of district-level employee training sessions was held. During the second year of implementation, a Core Values Workshop for Parents was developed and delivered upon request by schools.

## A Community Called to Action

The Mayor's Task Force on Community Values was initiated in response to the July 29, 1994 shootings of a doctor and an escort at a local abortion clinic. As a result of the shootings, Pensacola was thrust into the national media spotlight. Mayor John Fogg called together a cross-section of individuals from the community who reviewed local and national programs that offer assistance in conflict resolution. The Task Force members agreed that developing a set of community core values could be the rallying point needed in this time of crisis.

CorVal, Inc. was called upon again to facilitate this process. Seven community values were adopted: nonviolence, respect, integrity, hope, justice, community pride, and faith. Following the work of the Mayor's Task Force on Community Values, several training sessions were held for representatives of the Escambia County School District, the Pensacola Area Chamber of Commerce, Gulf Power Company, and other interested individuals.

In February 1995, the Mayor's Task Force, in conjunction with representatives from the school district, military community, businesses, and churches held a Community Values Campaign Kick-Off at the National Museum of Naval Aviation. The school district agreed to join the community effort through increased awareness and activities in the entire school community.

An outgrowth from the Mayor's Task Force has been the Community Core Values Board chaired by retired Vice Admiral Jack Fetterman, U.S. Navy. This group of individuals meets monthly to discuss community issues related to values, communications and involvement. The board serves as the catalyst for keeping core values in the forefront of the community through speaking engagements and sponsorship of community activities. The mission of the group is to make the slogan "Pensacola: A Values-Based Community" a reality.

Superintendent Maloy, Vice Admiral Jack Fetterman, and Dr. Tom McQueen of CorVal, Inc. were invited to make a presentation at the National Conference on Ethics in America, outlining the combined efforts of the community and the schools.

## Empowering Students

In March 1995, the first Building Your Vision Leadership Seminar was sponsored by the Core Values Awareness Committee. More than 200 high school students were invited to hear a keynote address by Clayton King, a dynamic speaker for the National Beta Club. Following the general assembly, the students attended their choices from seven breakout sessions which focused on topics such as diversity, communications, team building, community service and critical thinking. Over 70 students signed up to form a District Core Values Team which began plans for future student activities in the district.

Some members of the Core Values Team participated in a special three-hour training session to prepare them for making presentations in elementary school classrooms. During the training session, the Core Values Team reviewed the six core values and learned simple teaching tips, practiced with the lessons, stories and materials, and viewed a videotape of a second grade teacher modeling a core values lesson. The classroom lessons and materials were developed by the Core Values Writing Team, a group of teachers representing all grades and disciplines.

In addition to meeting monthly, the Core Values Team also participates in community service activities. They have volunteered their time at the Gulf Coast Arts Festival, Heritage Festival, Holocaust Remembrance,

Family Expo, Core Values Media Breakfast and other community events. Members have served as official ambassadors for the school district at special activities. Many of them started teams at their own schools; other members brought the core values message to existing organizations such as the Student Government Association or National Honor Society.

The Core Values Awareness Committee, along with the student team, has continued to sponsor the "Building Your Vision" Leadership Seminar for the past two years, expanding the invitation to middle schoolers to attend. The Core Values Team has also sponsored a rock concert, the "Core Values Concert in the Square," as a way to heighten awareness and recruit new members.

As the students have become more involved in the district effort, they have designed their own team logo, a peeling apple with the core values printed on it, and the slogan "Core Values are Appealing!" T-shirts, buttons, and book bags are provided to the team members to enhance recognition of their efforts.

To collaborate with the community board, Core Values Team members were paired with community leaders to say in their own words what each of the values meant to them. The statements were video- and audiotaped and provided to the local media for use in a media campaign.

## Teachers in Action

Key to the success of the core values initiative are the activities of the classroom teachers. The Core Values Writing Team was so enthusiastic that, in addition to developing the materials for use by the Core Values Team in the elementary schools, they produced a 300-plus page Core Values Activity Book. There were two main concepts in the preparation of the book: the core values program is not an add-on to the curriculum, and the lessons and materials must be "teacher-friendly" and easily accessible. The book includes lesson plans and reference materials for teachers at all grade levels and in all disciplines.

The Core Values Awareness Committee hosted a special book debut at the local Books-a-Million at which time the books were distributed free to all teachers who attended and T-shirts were provided to the Writing Team for their efforts. Copies of the book have been distributed to all schools and special centers. The Core Values Writing Team has committed to writing and publishing a Core Values Activity Book for Parents during the 1997-98 school year.

# A Shot in the Arm

During the third year of implementation, the Core Values Awareness Committee decided that the district effort needed a "shot in the arm." Speakers had been invited in to address students during school assemblies about core values. Community organizations such as the Rotary Clubs and Friends of the Library had helped by making class presentations, providing coloring books and music cassettes, sponsoring a core values essay contest, and hosting the first Annual Core Values Student Recognition Luncheon. Businesses like the Herff Jones Company, First Union Bank, Gulf Power Company and Cox Communications were providing financial support for core values activities. What was needed was a dynamic individual who could rally all the forces together, bringing a unified effort to the initiative.

At this time Dr. Philip Vincent was conducting a workshop in Orlando based on his book, *Developing Character in Students*. A committee reviewed the outline of the seminar and decided that his approach was one that could easily be brought into the existing effort.

Representatives from the district attended a two-day seminar and came back with rave reviews. Dr. Vincent was then invited to present a district-wide seminar for all school teams. He spoke to 200 participants at the "Community Address on Core Values" and presented a workshop for the faculty and students at Washington High School.

Following these initial presentations, Dr. Vincent was invited back by Pensacola High School, Wedgewood Middle School, Weis Elementary School, and Hallmark Elementary School. Many of the schools have included core values in their school improvement plans and there is evidence that more activities are taking place at the schools which focus on core values.

# What's Next?

In November 1996, Jim May was elected as superintendent of schools. He is committed to continue the core values efforts with emphasis placed on the classroom. All of the committees will continue to expand their efforts.

A special two-day "Rising STARS Challenge" was scheduled for early in the 1997-98 school year focusing on middle school students. (STARS is an acronym for Successful, Talented and Responsible Students.) These students were challenged to learn about core values, conflict resolution, community service, job ethics, motivation, and peer pressure, and to develop a team effort at their schools. To give them necessary support, an adult volunteer was asked to commit to a year-long involvement with the students in planning school activities and team projects. Graduates of the Challenge received t-shirts, buttons and certificates identifying them as STARS. The students were joined by the Pensacola Ice Pilots Hockey Team at their graduation ceremony.

Formative and summative evaluations of the middle school efforts will be conducted to determine the effectiveness of this approach in implementing core values.

The success of this initiative, like any other, is dependent on the people who are involved. The members of the various committees, the students on the Core Values Team, and the individuals in classrooms committed to modeling ethical behaviors and influencing others to do the same thing, are crucial to the successful implementation of the school district's core values program. A winning combination is to pair administrative leadership and school support with community and parental buy-in and involvement.

While the Escambia County School District has made strides in the area of core values that we are very proud of, there is still much to do. The old story about how to eat a whale—one bite at a time—is applicable in this instance. If even one student modifies his or her behavior by believing that core values are important, that is success.

To build on our current efforts, the Core Values Awareness Committee is developing a web site, planning to expand programs in the middle schools, continuing to collect research and other materials related to core values, and expanding collaboration with community organizations. The Escambia County School District will continue to do its part to make Pensacola a truly values-based community.

# $\mathcal{5}$ANSON COUNTY, NC

## *"Dream It! Believe It! Be It!"*
## *Building Character Each Day*
## *at Lilesville Elementary School*

**Steve Dixon**
Principal, Lilesville Elementary School

## ▓ Character Education: A Catalyst for Change

Lilesville Elementary School, a K-6 school located in rural Anson County, North Carolina, has an enrollment of 410 pupils. Over 65% of the students qualify for free or reduced meal service. The school system is identified as a "low wealth" school system due to the limited degree of local funding for schools. Despite the seemingly disadvantaged conditions, in 1997 and 1998 the school has earned an "exemplary" rating on the North Carolina ABCs of Public Education, a state ranking system based on student improvement on the North Carolina end-of-grade test in reading and mathematics. Schools earning the exemplary rating have shown student growth in tested grades of at least 110% of expected growth for the year. Known locally for our vision, our school has a site-based decision-making policy, and we are comfortable piloting change agent-type initiatives. A school mission statement established in 1988 states:

> *Lilesville Elementary School is committed to the belief that all children can learn. Our mission is to teach each child to levels of mastery learning and encourage behaviors and attitudes that prepare them to be productive citizens.*

With a belief that students should be "productive citizens," it was only natural that after the site-based management team met Dr. Philip Vincent of the Character Development Group during a sharing visit to a neighboring school system that Lilesville staff would want to hear more about character development. We invited Dr. Vincent to conduct an orientation session in June 1997. During the summer all staff used Dr. Vincent's *Developing Character in Students* and the accompanying workbook to prepare for our program. The first session was followed by a second session in August 1997. This session permitted the staff to fine-tune the initiatives discussed in the first session and to formulate processes. These two sessions launched our schoolwide character development program.

## Year One: The Dream Becomes a Belief

With two sessions by Dr. Vincent providing a framework to begin, the school staff agreed on six character traits that would be taught and modeled by the school community. Those traits were:
- Respect
- Responsibility
- Caring
- Trustworthiness
- Fairness
- Citizenship

One trait would be emphasized during each of the six grading periods, as well as collectively throughout the year. Believing as we do that strength comes from teamwork, every member of the school community shared in the commitment to teach and model these traits. Teachers, administrators, teacher assistants, bus drivers, food service employees and custodians—all of whom had participated in Dr. Vincent's training sessions—were regularly involved in planning for our character development program.

# Growing Character One Child at a Time

Year one saw a transition toward a better moral climate throughout the school. Respect, responsibility and caring became a part of our regular vocabulary. Lilesville staff members modeled the character traits that they sought to cultivate in the students. Children began to notice when their classmates were showing respect and behaving responsibly, *and when they were not.*

Being a schoolwide initiative has been a definite strength. Students and parents have heard character themes in classrooms, on buses, in the cafeteria, at PTA meetings—even from the custodians concerning school cleanliness.

Character has become contagious! Students can be heard saying "Please," "Thank you," "Yes, Ma'am," and "No, Sir" with regularity all around the school. Student conflicts have been minimal and teachers feel invigorated by the better school climate. Putting character first has been the best thing we could have done for our kids.

# The Five Elements of Character Development: A Road Map for Change

A belief by the school staff that character education should not be just an add-on, but integrated into the everyday life at school was important. It led to the adoption of the Five Spokes of Character Development that would move the character education program from a belief to a reality at Lilesville Elementary School. Those spokes are:

**Rules and Procedures:** The staff developed a set of both general and specific rules that would govern the school community. Those rules were:

*General Rules:*
1. We will respect others and their property.
2. We will be honest, responsible, polite and caring.
3. We will follow directions when given.

*Specific Rules:*
1. Be in class on time with all needed materials.
2. Raise hands and wait to be recognized.
3. Keep hands, feet and objects to oneself.
4. Always walk in an orderly fashion on the right.
5. Use only appropriate language (no vulgar, profane or offensive words or gestures).

These rules and procedures were the basis for communicating clearly to our students what we expected as appropriate behavior. The staff utilized class meetings and lessons to establish what these rules "looked like." Classes compiled lists of procedures that students could follow to help them "learn" how to be respectful, responsible, caring students.

**Cooperative Learning Opportunities:** Staff at our school felt quite comfortable with this component due to previous staff development opportunities. The classroom climate was one where cooperative learning was frequently used. Students were familiar with various team roles. Teachers understood the importance of using cooperative learning opportunities to teacher students how to share, support, lead, follow and take turns.

**Character-Rich Classroom Literature:** Books and stories with themes that addressed character traits such as respect, responsibility, caring, trustworthiness, fairness and citizenship were used regularly. The character bibliography from Burlington City Schools was used as a resource. Stories such as those found in *The Book of Virtues* and *The Children's Book of Virtues,* compiled by William J. Bennett, became an important resource.

**Teaching for Thinking:** Thinking was treated as a skill to be taught. Students were taught to sequence and order their thoughts. Thinking maps and graphic organizers were used frequently in class activities. Students were asked to determine the right decisions one would make to exhibit good character.

**Service Learning:** Students were encouraged to volunteer in and out of the school. Numerous service projects that would help students model character traits were developed for classrooms, for grade levels and for the entire school.

## Character Development Activities That Helped Us "Be It"!

We came up with dozens of ideas for activities that would enhance our teaching of individual character traits and would keep the idea of developing good character in front of the students every day. Here are some of the best ideas:

- **Character Traits Displays**—All classrooms highlighted character traits throughout the year in colorful displays of student artwork, essays, poetry and models.

- **Character Banners**—Large banners stating the six key character traits were displayed in the school's dining hall.
- **Class Meetings**—Teachers began their day with a routine that in cluded a 5- to 10-minute discussion about what various character traits "look like." Students and teachers used these sessions to talk about character building and to develop classroom procedures to built character.
- **Parent Workshops**—Teachers sponsored four evening sessions with parents. PTA leaders met with groups of parents at various grade levels and shared techniques they used with their own kids to promote respect and responsibility.
- **"Caught Showing Character" Recognition Program**—School staff nominated students each week when they observed them dem onstrating respect, responsibility and caring habits at school. Students nominated were recognized via the school intercom and awarded with ribbons indicating that they were "caught showing good character."
- **Essay/Drawing Contests**—Each six weeks students were invited to submit essays and drawings that addressed the character trait for that period. Topics such as "What does respect look like?" and "What does a caring person look like?" etc. gave students the op portunity to draw or write on the subject. Drawings were displayed in the main hallway and essay winners read their essays over the school intercom.
- **Shipshape Battleship Restoration**—Students were encouraged to participate in the restoration campaign for the U.S.S. *North Carolina* Battleship Memorial in Wilmington, North Carolina. A special field trip to the battleship memorial was a scheduled to allow participating students to submit their contributions personally.
- **Cans for Kids Food Drive**—Students donated over 3,000 cans of food to the Anson Crisis Ministry during the Christmas season.
- **Tools for School**—The school counselor coordinated a school supplies bureau for children needing them. Students, families and area businesses were encouraged to donate school supplies such as pencils, pens, paper, crayons, notebooks and bookbags.
- **Kiwanis Club Terrific Kids**—The local service club sponsored a breakfast for students who demonstrated good character. Each six weeks the students were recognized with certificates, buttons, and school supplies. Parents were invited to attend the breakfast along with their child.

## Character Development: A Journey, Not a Destination

At the end of the 1997-98 school year, all staff members at Lilesville completed the Character Development Group's Character Assessment Checklist, an instrument that evaluates the level of implementation of a character education program. Results of the assessment were the basis for a third session with Dr. Vincent at the opening of the 1998-99 school year. The results validated the importance of continued refinement of a moral climate at our school. Now we will focus on creating greater involvement of students in leadership roles to give them an opportunity to showcase good character traits. Also, we are considering more effective ways to communicate to parents the expectations of our program. More service learning projects, both by grade levels and schoolwide, are being planned.

Character development is a journey, not a destination. Students need teachers, parents and community leaders to be moral compasses to help lead them to become rich in character. Character education is not something you "do" and then say, "We've done character education." It must become the way you do everything at your school.

*"To educate a person in mind and not in morals is to educate a menace to society."*
—Theodore Roosevelt

# *6* LIVERPOOL, NY

## Morgan Road Elementary's Character Education Story

### Richard Parisi
Principal, Morgan Road Elementary School

## 🔳 Getting Started

Morgan Road is a K-6 building of approximately 450 students in the Liverpool Central School District. Liverpool is located in Central New York and is a suburb of Syracuse. Late in the 1991-1992 year, the staff was looking at our building discipline policies. It was decided to make some changes in what we were doing and to evaluate this during the next year. Despite many students who showed responsible and respectful behaviors, we were seeing a growing number of students who did not. Our evaluation process showed us that the changes we had made were not getting to the root of problems. That issue was the character development of our students.

Because of this concern, nine members of the Cooperative Planning Team (CPT), the site-based team at Morgan Road Elementary School, attended a one-day conference on Character Education in November 1994.

The keynote speaker was Dr. Thomas Lickona, a professor at S.U.N.Y. Cortland, and a national leader in character education. He mentioned that the two great purposes of public education in America had always been to help develop academic abilities and the positive character qualities that would be needed to be contributing members of a democratic society. Dr. Lickona shared a list that he called "Ten Troubling Trends Which Point to the Need for Character Education." It was our concern about some of these trends which had prompted our signing up for the conference. The Ten Trends he presented are:

1. Rising youth violence
2. Increasing dishonesty (lying, cheating, and stealing)
3. Growing disrespect for parents, teachers and other legitimate authorityfigures
4. Increasing peer cruelty
5. A rise in prejudice and hate crime
6. The deterioration of language
7. A decline in work ethic
8. Declining personal and civic responsibility
9. Increasing self-destructive behaviors such as premature sexual activity, substance abuse and suicide
10. Growing ethical illiteracy, including ignorance of moral knowledge as basic as the Golden Rule, and the tendency to engage in destructive behavior

The nine members of our CPT who had attended the conference shared their impressions with those who had not been able to attend, and their enthusiasm about what they had learned was contagious. At the December meeting we decided we wanted to move ahead with the study of character education. During his talk Dr. Lickona mentioned the Center for the Fourth and Fifth Rs, Respect and Responsibility, which had just been established at S.U.N.Y Cortland. He also mentioned that the Center would be hosting its first Summer Institute on Character Education. Our planning team decided to send a team to the Summer Institute on Character Education. The six people who signed up to go were excited about the opportunity to spend a week in Cortland hearing about the philosophy of character education as well as practical tips to help in getting started.

Our team was made up of four teachers, a parent representative, and the building principal. To maximize the effectiveness of any school's character education program, it is critically important that staff, parents and administration are all committed to the chosen initiatives. Staff are critical because they are the day-to-day contacts and models for children. Their commitment and willingness to look at new ways to approach issues is the foundation of your program. For students to internalize core ethical values, there needs to be a strong home-school connection. Administrative support can help to provide the finances, time, and encouragement that are needed to develop a comprehensive character education program.

## Deciding on Character Goals

Once we agreed to move forward we began to examine articles, books, and existing programs to decide on the goals of our program. For the staff we purchased Dr. Lickona's *Educating for Character: How our Schools Can Teach Respect and Responsibility* and our planning team discussed several articles on character education. One of the best was "The Eleven Principles of Effective Character Education" by Tom Lickona, Eric Schaps and Catherine Lewis. The first principle they discussed was that character education promotes core ethical values as the basis of good character. They stated that there were certain core ethical values, such as caring, honesty and responsibility that form the basis of good character.

After meeting with the CPT and staff, we chose to become a member of the Character Counts Coalition, which is part of the Josephson Institute. We had several reasons for doing so:

- Our mission statement is: Morgan Road Elementary is a Caring, Cooperative Community Dedicated to Learning. (Caring is one of the six core values of the Character Counts Coalition.)
- Our staff had been talking about the 3Rs—Rules, Respect and Responsibility—for a number of years and two of the core values from Character Counts were respect and responsibility.
- We agreed that the other three values were ones we could work on with our students, families and staff. Those were trustworthiness, fairness and citizenship.
- Character Counts provided us with resources that made our job easier. We received posters, newsletters, curriculum materials and videos.
- We thought being a part of a national organization that was trying to make a difference for children and families in regards to character development would be exciting.

Our CPT developed our Morgan Road Character Education Building. The illustration includes the six pillars from Character Counts, as well as our mission statement. The Golden Rule forms the base of our building.

## Knowing, Loving, and Doing the Good

"Knowing the good, loving the good, and doing the good" is a basic goal for character education. We decided it was important that we provide opportunities for our students to gain head, heart and hand knowledge about doing the good. Most of our students had head knowledge about core values such as respect and responsibility. However, many did not love the good or consistently do the good. Our goal is to help students move from knowing (head) to loving (heart) to doing (hand) the good both in and outside of school.

During the last three years we have planned a number of activities to help our students move to the level of doing the good. However, the starting point was to make sure we were all together in terms of core values that we believed were important. One of the first things we did was to plan a school-wide assembly. Each grade level was responsible for highlighting their core value. Students used a variety of methods to present their character pillar (core values) such as skits, poetry, songs and dance. For example, grade five did a number of short skits on trustworthiness, grade six did an acrostic on citizenship, and grade two did a cheer about respect.

The CPT developed a calendar for when we would focus on each of our six pillars, and each grade level was assigned a core value for which it would have a primary responsibility. They chose some special activity that would help highlight that value for the entire community. Teachers at all levels were looking for ways to integrate character pillars into their curriculum.

Each fall the building principal has grade-level assemblies and one of the themes stressed is the importance of each core value. This may be reinforced by reading books such as Marcus Pfister's *Rainbow Fish to the Rescue* or articles from "Heroes For Today" found in *Reader's Digest*. These values are then reinforced by staff as they begin to meet with students and develop expectations for the year. Posters of Morgan Road's Character Ed Building were distributed to staff members and are displayed as visual reminders. The examples mentioned so far are just a few of the ways that we used to help students begin to know the good.

# Building-wide Projects

Structuring opportunities so students can learn to love and do the good is key to a successful program. We have "Buddy Classes" with three-year age spans. Students have read together, co-authored books, worked in the courtyard, and celebrated special events. One second and one fifth grade class worked on a wonderful "Friendship Quilt" with a parent volunteer. It was displayed at the New York State Fair with a description of what their classes had done during the year. A third grade and a kindergarten teacher worked together and had a "High Pillar Friendship Tea" and celebrated all they had done during the year to develop friendships. Students dressed up for this special event, which included musicians, skits, songs and poems that reinforced core virtues. There also was plenty of good food including a cake which read "High Pillar Friendship Tea."

Another opportunity for our students, parents and staff to work together as "a caring, cooperative community dedicated to learning" is our Giving Tree Project. This began a number of years ago as a hat-and-mitten drive with gifts going to a local charity. Since beginning our more comprehensive character education program, we have expanded the Giving Tree so that we are helping approximately twenty families and more than forty children from our school. This project begins in October with a school-wide bottle drive to raise funds. It continues with a food drive in November and a gift drive in December. Two staff members begin shopping for the next year on December 26th and items are added throughout the year. The PTO also donates funds every year to support the program. This year two staff members planned a staff-versus-parents volleyball challenge for the Giving Tree. Everyone had a great time as we raised money for a good cause.

We have a wonderful courtyard at Morgan Road that was developed with staff, parents and students working together. One of our parents, a landscape architect, helped us decide how our courtyard area could be used to promote academic and character growth. The students met with him and worked in cooperative groups to design a bird sanctuary which they then helped to plant and maintain. The students also worked with staff and parents to bring in topsoil and to do initial plantings. During the last two years several staff members started a garden club of fourth, fifth and sixth graders who met after school in the fall and spring to do a variety of projects connected to the courtyard. The courtyard has had academic benefits in terms of science, writing and art projects. It has also provided hands-on opportunities for students to demonstrate character traits such as responsibility, caring, respect, trustworthiness, and good citizenship. Remember, it is our goal that our students will go from head to heart to hand knowledge so they are actually doing the good.

## Community Projects

One of our Girl Scout leaders asked if her Brownie troop could do a school-wide book drive to support students in a city school. Our students brought in so many books we were able to provide more than one book per student. In addition to bringing in the books, students worked to count, separate, box and deliver the books.

Two years ago the Liverpool School District began a special luncheon program for senior citizens. When it was our turn to host the seniors, our fourth graders sang for them and our fifth and sixth graders made placemats for over 170 people. Our sixth graders also worked with older students to serve lunch and clean up after the luncheon. Many of those attending commented on the responsible and respectful attitudes of the students. Our children were doing something to provide for others and learning that it felt good to do so.

Visiting nursing homes or malls to perform for others is something that instrumental music groups have done. They have received thank-you notes from many of those they visited.

After a family's tragic house fire in January 1998 our students, parents, community members, and staff responded in a powerful way. After our request for help, boxes of clothes, food, toys and books came in. Staff, parents, and the PTO also contributed funds. Families in the community heard of our efforts and made donations. Several people donated furniture and appliance items. At a PTO Family Bingo Night, additional cash donations were made. We shared the need with other schools in our district and they contributed through their student councils or directly from their staff. It really became a full community effort. When thanked for donating furniture one parent replied, "It's just treating others the way you would like to be treated."

## Grade-Level Projects

Each month a grade level was responsible for leading our efforts on a different core value. It has been fun to see the different ideas students and staff have come up with. For example, second graders doing announcements about respect all during February, or an assembly where they did songs and a cheer, and presented a big book about respect. Second graders also worked with fifth graders to do a play, "The Empty Pot," which highlighted trustworthiness. Fifth graders wrote about what it meant to be a trustworthy person and shared their thoughts over the morning announcements. In January 1998 a group of fifth graders worked together to do a bulletin board on trustworthiness. Fourth graders did fairness skits in cooperative groups and videotaped them for the school. In a previous year they had done a bulletin board on fairness where they wrote and illustrated a scene which showed fairness. It was exciting to see students thinking about ways they could demonstrate one of the virtues.

During the 1996-1997 year, grade 6 developed a form asking if any staff would like student volunteers to help in their rooms. There was a tremendous response from staff. Students began to work as reading partners, math tutors, physical education helpers, computer tutors and office workers.They helped with the buses, announcements, distribution of materials, and many other activities. These student volunteers gave up their recess times up to three times a week to help others. This focus on citizenship was for October, but many continued to volunteer for the entire year. Dr. Martin Luther King, Jr. said, "Life's most persistent and urgent question is: What are you doing for others?" It was exciting to see our sixth graders doing for others throughout the entire year.

## Classroom Projects

Community, schoolwide, and grade-level projects are all important parts of our character education program. However, without classroom projects the program will never have the impact we desire. James Baldwin declared, "Children have never been good at listening to their elders, but they have never failed to imitate them." There are interactions in classrooms each day where staff members are able to model good character for their students. The expectations they set for student behaviors are a critical piece of a total program.

One of the most common approaches used by teachers is to have students connect core virtues to selections from literature they are reading. For example, one third grade class read one of the Boxcar Children books and looked for ways characters demonstrated different virtues. The students then wrote about these characters and displayed their writing on a bulletin board train. A sixth grade teacher shared a number of picture books. The students discussed the core virtues that were highlighted in the books. They did a writing activity on the computer where they developed a slide show presentation about their books. Our librarian has developed a list of books that are connected to each virtue which she distributes to all staff prior to the start of a new month to help teachers select read-alouds related to that month's core virtue.

One of our kindergarten teachers has made signs for each core virtue and has students hold one up prior to activities which would demonstrate that virtue. For example, cleaning up after a play time would be a time when a student would hold up the RESPONSIBILITY sign. Helping a student learn to tie his shoes would be a time to display the CARING sign.

Our music, art, library and physical education teachers all have many opportunities to work on character development. One example was a winter concert where the Fourth Grade Chorus worked together with the art and music teacher to do a program, "Lovin' Kindness," which featured songs related to character development. They also worked together to bring in "Vitamin L," a student singing group whose songs include character-building messages. Students learned these songs in their music classes and many also sang them in their classrooms. We played a number of them over the daily announcements.

Our fourth, fifth, and sixth grade teachers participated in the National Mock Presidential Election in 1996. They taught short lessons in their classes and provided opportunities for the students to vote. The students were involved in carrying out the tasks necessary to have a successful election.

During November 1996, the first grade teachers served the Thanksgiving lunch to all their students in their classrooms. The students loved eating in their rooms and the teachers modeled one way of caring for others. They also wrote about "Caring Kids" with their Buddy Classes.

## Parent Connections

We believe that, to have an effective program, teachers have to work hand in hand with our parents. Right from the beginning, we've had parents involved through our CPT and PTO. After attending the Summer Institute at Cortland with staff, some parents helped to design a form which shared our ideas about getting involved in a comprehensive approach to character development. The form described the core virtues we would focus on and asked parents to express any questions or concerns. One parent felt teaching character should be entirely the parents' responsibility. We spoke with that parent and agreed that parents are the key moral educators of their children. We came to agreement that we could all be more successful in this area if we worked together on core values we agreed were important.

Once parents were aware of our plans and wanted us to move forward, we had to find ways to keep them informed and involved in activities that could make a difference for them and their children. During the first year of the program, the monthly Message From the Principal always included information about the virtue of the month. It might include inspirational quotes, suggestions or activities that families could do to work on that attribute. Grade levels took the responsibility of doing a monthly family calendar on the virtue, which included ideas that would reinforce the concept.

Our CPT continued to work on character development and brought in Dr. Lickona to speak to parents from across our school district. They worked with all of the parent organizations to set up this special evening. Parents from our CPT also spoke to other parents about the importance of character development at our Back to School Night in the fall. They gave updates on what we had been working on and some of our goals. CPT members also wrote newsletter articles about character education. Our site-based team began working on an informational brochure which discussed our overall school program. One section highlighted our character education program. Several times a year CPT members would give brief updates at PTO meetings.

We also used students to connect with parents through special activities. In one such activity, each student received a strip of paper for parents to fill out ways their children were demonstrating responsibility at home or in the community. When they were returned the third grade made a large "More Responsibility Everywhere" bulletin board. We became involved in the "TV Turn-off Week." Parents and students were asked to share ways that they spent the extra time they had from turning off the television. We made a bulletin board that listed these ideas. Another example of connecting with our families was having our students sing special thank you songs to our parents at the PTO Appreciation Tea. Our music teacher recruited students from each classroom and they were a big hit with the parents who attended. Students also wrote thank you notes, made paper flowers, and place mats. The staff supplied the food along with additional thank-you notes.

## Assessing Our Program

At the end of the first year we conducted a brief survey of our parents, receiving forms from approximately one third of our families. In answering the survey questions, 96% of the families agreed or strongly agreed that they understood the purpose of the character education program and 94% that character education could assist them in positively affecting their child's education. Also, 74% reported that they used the monthly character education calendars sometimes or frequently. Parents reported that 70% of the children were talking about character education sometimes or frequently at home. We were pleased to see that parents were aware of our program and that it was being discussed at home. Tools like the calendar were being used by a large majority of families. We were most pleased that 94% agreed that character education could positively assist them in their child's education.

We also asked in what areas of the student's life they would most like to see character education explored. The largest numbers responded that the classroom and school bus environments were of the most interest. As a result of that feedback, we continue to focus on character in the classroom. The building principal has begun to hold annual meetings with the transportation team to explain our program and to look at ways to improve bus behavior so it is consistent with our character goals. Drivers have received packets about the program. Each month they receive a poster with the virtue of the month to be displayed in their buses.

At the end of the first year, teachers were asked to fill out a brief survey developed by our planning team. At a staff meeting, we made decisions about program modifications. For example, we extended our focus on Caring to two months in November and December because it fit in so well with our Giving Tree Project. We also decided to continue "The No Putdowns Program." Each grade level kept its own core value so that over the years a student would be responsible for different ones.

## Sustaining Enthusiasm

We have an experienced staff which has seen many programs come and go over the years. One of our concerns was how to maintain enthusiasm and improve what we're doing in character education. One strategy is to stay in contact with others who can help us to continue growing. We've had staff members attend the Summer Institute on Character Education each of the last three years to gain new ideas. Staff members have also attended one-day seminars during the year with Dr. Lickona at The Center For the Fourth and Fifth Rs. We have brought in staff trainers this year to help us learn more about morning meetings and cooperative learning. We've also sent seven staff members to a two-day training by Spencer Kagan on "Multiple Intelligences and Cooperative Learning."

One of the biggest steps we took to make sure the program kept moving forward was establishing a Character and Reading Enrichment (CARE) Committee. Because our planning team has moved on to a new goal, we knew we needed a group to help us keep focus on the importance of character development. Members met for three half days over the summer to start planning for the 1997-1998 year. They decided to meet monthly during the school year. One of the events planned was a special kick-off celebration for the opening staff meeting this year where the theme of "Hearts and Hands Making a Difference at Morgan Road" was introduced. When students returned to school the front windows and doors were covered with hearts and hands. During the next few days in art classes, students traced their own hands and then added a heart. These were used to make a chain down the main hallway and reminded everyone of our theme. Posters were made for each classroom and the lobby. Keeping visual reminders before students, parents and staff is another way to remind people about the importance of our program.

We decided to link character and reading in our CARE group because we felt it was an important and natural connection. We want our character efforts to be integrated into the curriculum. Reading, discussing and writing about literature, history, science, art and music are all great ways to encourage character development in children. Our goal was to link the two great goals of American public education, academic learning and the development of positive character qualities.

## Future Steps

For Morgan Road Elementary, character education is here to stay. It's not a two- or three-year program. We're planning staff development to continue improving our skills in cooperative learning. We also want to reach out to our teacher aides, custodians and transportation team to insure we're working toward common goals.

Providing opportunities for students to get more involved in leadership roles like special councils and peer mediation is an area to work on.

We also want to help strengthen students' inner character resources: moral reasoning, self-control, and strategies for responsible behavior in the future. We also want to assess our students' progress in developing an emotional attachment and commitment to the qualities of good character.

Getting students consistently to choose to do the good and help others is hard work, but it will improve their classroom learning environment and pay dividends for their future. As Dr. Martin Luther King, Jr. said, "We must remember that intelligence is not enough. Intelligence plus character—that is the true goal of education." We need to persist in our efforts to help children develop both as learners and as people of character.

# 7 WINSTON-SALEM, NC

---

# Our Character Education Program at Rural Hall Elementary School

**Carole E. Rosenbaum**
Primary Reading Teacher
Chairman, Character Education Committee

**Fonda Rosenbaum**
Physical Education Specialist
Character Education Committee

## ▓ MISSION STATEMENT

*The Winston-Salem/Forsyth County School System takes joint responsibility with families, religious organizations, and the community in building character in young people.*

## Developing Our Program

The administration of Winston-Salem/Forsyth County Schools selected a group of forty educators and community leaders to form a Character Education Committee. The committee's purpose was to develop a mission statement and to declare the focus, outcomes and statement of roles for character education in our school system.

Staff development training by Dr. Philip Fitch Vincent was offered to faculty groups from each school to assist them in developing a character education plan. Bill Moser, a member of this original committee, was selected to be our school system's Health/Character Education Program Specialist.

The teachers and staff at Rural Hall readily agreed that character education should be integrated into our daily routine, not an add-on program. WE DID NOT WANT ANOTHER CURRICULUM TO TEACH! Many teachers already focused on character, but we could have greater impact if we set a common goal. We would benefit from sharing ideas and learning from each other, and we could accomplish more if we all used the same terms and definitions throughout the school.

Our entire staff uses the COET (Classroom Organization for Effective Teaching) Program. This program ties in well with character education because COET stresses the importance of modeling behavior, focusing on positive character traits, and holding high expectations for the students. All of our school adults and students work together to create a conducive environment for learning.

## First Year—1996-1997

The Character Education Committee worked to establish guidelines and to suggest activities, programs, and other resources. This committee consisted of teachers, guidance counselors, the principal, and assistant principal. Consensus was reached on a mission statement and which character traits we would emphasize. These were published in a brochure sent to educators, students, parents, and community groups. The mission statement is at the beginning of this essay. The selected traits were:

**Caring**
**Courage**
**Integrity**
**Perseverance**
**Respect**
**Responsibility**
**Self-Discipline**

Following are some of the strategies we implemented during the first focused year of character education:

- **Emphasis for the Month**—One of the seven character traits was emphasized each month and announced on the intercom daily. That trait was featured in a bulletin board display in the main hall.
- **Thought for the Week**—Each week we presented a motivational thought that correlated with the trait of the month. This thought was also announced each morning on the intercom. Some examples:
  Never settle for less than your best.
  If you want to make your dreams come true, don't oversleep!
  If you don't stand for something, you'll fall for anything.
  It's the little things in life that determine the big things.
  Doing right is more important than being right.
- **Students of the Week**—One student in each classroom was chosen to be the "Student of the Week" based on behavior we wished to encourage. These students' names were announced each Monday morning and were posted in the halls. On Fridays, the Students of the Week came to the lobby for special recognition. They were given certificates and photographed for the local newspaper and school scrapbook. They also received coupons for treats or activities from local businesses.
- **Banners and posters**—PTA funds were used to buy banners and posters that promoted character education. These were displayed in the halls, classrooms, and cafeteria. Students were attracted to these colorful displays and frequently were observed reading them. Even very young students could recite the sayings and explain you what they meant.
- **Character Education Scrapbook**—Photographs of the Students of the Week were compiled in a scrapbook, along with photographs of special bulletin boards and activities. The scrapbook was on display in the school lobby for students, parents, and visitors to see.
- **Activity File**—Teachers were asked to share any successful teaching tools, ideas, activities, books, or videos with their stu dents.
- **Resource Center**—Media Center staff designated an area to keep all character education materials. Books, book lists, videos, and re-source guides were stored together for easy checkout.
- **Special Programs**—Our Special Events Committee scheduled several programs. Two of these were the Athletes' Care Team from Wake Forest University and the North Carolina Demonstration Jump Rope Team. Both these groups talked to the children about self-discipline, perseverance, caring, and other character traits.

- **Service Projects**—Our school had several projects to show that our students are "Kids That Care." We made tray favors for the American Red Cross to send to local nursing homes. A clothing and housewares drive was held for one of our families when their home was destroyed by fire. Over $7700 was raised in our 16th Annual Jump Rope for Heart Event. A fund was set up to raise money for a North Dakota school that had been devastated by the floods. Our school participated in the Clean and Green Beautification Program and a recycling program. Several service projects were completed by individual classes.
- **Thought for the Week Patrol**—Faculty members would occasionally wear a silly hat with a big sign on it saying "Do you know the thought for the week?" They would go into classrooms randomly and give small rewards to the students who knew the current Thought for the Week.
- **Literature**—Teachers used stories in our basal reading program that correlated with our selected character traits.

## Second Year—1997-1998

Since our first year was so successful at building faculty interest and involvement, we decided to expand our program with additional new ideas. The following are some of our schoolwide activities:

- **Character Education Week**—Our school system designated one week as "Character Education Week." Special activities were planned by our school.
- **Character Education Boxes**—One of our business partners designed for us large boxes with one of the character traits printed on them. They are on display in our lobby and teachers use them as teaching tools in their classrooms.
- **Pep Rally**—The entire student body attended a pep rally about positive character traits. Students from our Presidential Council marched into the gym carrying Character Education Boxes. Each announced his trait and gave a short definition to the audience, then a pyramid was built with the boxes. Wake Forest University cheerleaders led some cheers, and individuals explained to the students how each trait had been important in their lives.
- **"Kids That Care" Coat Drive**—Students donated 211 coats, which were cleaned free by a dry cleaners and sent to the Sa vation Army.

- **School Newsletter**—Each issue of our newsletter contains an article informing parents of the character trait for the month and all related activities. We wanted to let them know what we were doing and encourage them to talk to their children about character, especially the trait we were emphasizing at the time.
- **Display of our Activities**—Photographs of activities and examples of children's work were set up on a large triptych in the lobby. The display and our scrapbook were exhibited at the lo cal school board meeting when character education was being dis cussed.
- **Surveys**—To evaluate our program, surveys were given to the staff. The results have been very helpful as we continue our focus on building character. Sample questions from the surveys include:

*For Students:*
  a. How do you see character education displayed at our  school?
  b. How has character education improved your relationship with teachers and students?
  c. What do you like about the "Student of the Week" program?
  d. How can we improve the character education program?

*For Teachers:*
  a. How has character education improved discipline in your classroom?
  b. What other benefits have you seen as a result of our character education program?

## Sharing Ideas and Activities

We have a schoolwide ACE program. The acronym stands for Attendance Conduct Effort. Students who make ACE are rewarded quarterly by going on special trips, having parties and other extra activities. Many of our teachers have changed the C to stand for character!

## Successful Classroom Activities

- Character traits and the Thought for the Week are discussed daily.
- Having the character traits posted in the classroom is very helpful and teachers refer to them often when discussing behavior.
- Role playing is an effective teaching tool. Teachers ask their students what they would do in various situations, focusing on choosing positive behavior to solve problems.

- "Character Walks" through the halls give students a chance to choose their favorite saying, write what it means to them and draw an illus tration of it.
- Students discuss the profiles and traits demonstrated by characters in literature. Some teachers use card pockets inside the back covers of books and the students are asked to list on the card the traits of the characters.
- All of our fifth graders took an overnight trip to Camp Thunderbird. The group activities and experiences focused on positive character traits. The ropes course encouraged team building, support, and cooperation. Courage, trust, perseverance, and self-discipline were discussed in the classes.
- Cooperative learning is used to encourage students to help each other.
- A Red Cross Drive is held one week each year to collect money.
- Some older and younger classes have become buddy classes. They visit each other's classrooms to read, present plays and skits, assist with activities, and have holiday parties.
- Students are urged to take responsibility for their own learning, their homework and notes to parents. Emphasis is placed on the student's responsibility for his actions and his responsibility when given tasks at school or home.
- School rules are posted in classrooms and in the halls. Students learn and review these rules in class discussions.
- A student will look up a character trait in the dictionary and read the definition to his classmates. The student has to interpret the definition, use the word in a sentence and give an example of that trait.
- During Social Studies activities, teachers discuss character traits of various people in current events and history.
- The names and photos of all Students of the Week are posted in the classrooms. Some classes "interview" that student and then make a class booklet and/or bulletin board about him. The class discusses the qualities of the student and why he was chosen.
- Some classes have composed mottos, such as the following:

> This very day, I'll do my best
> To work with pride and obey with zest.
> I will not waste my precious time
> Because there is learning to gain
> And the choice is mine!

- Booklets are made about individual character traits. Sample titles are: "When I Was Responsible," "What Respect Means To Me" and "I Was Courageous When I...."
- Thank-you notes are written to speakers and groups that come to our school to present programs.
- Our fifth graders participate in the DARE Program (Drug Abuse Resistance Education). This program stresses positive traits and making the right choices.
- During Christmas, door decorations were made for children's hospitals and shoe boxes of toys and supplies were sent to Franklin Graham's Shoebox Ministry.
- Students created inspirational thoughts to share with classmates.
- Some teachers taught lessons about the Kwanzaa principles: unity, self-determination, collective work and responsibility, purpose, creativity, and faith. Students could relate these traits to our character education traits.
- Students wrote letters to teachers, students and others expressing their appreciation and gratitude for the influence these people have had on their lives.
- When students are gathered and waiting for a late bus, no time is wasted. This is a teachable moment when word games can be played using the character traits.
- Students drew pictures of themselves portraying a particular character trait. These were taped together to make a paper quilt that was displayed in the halls.

## Successful Specialists' Activities

Although the general activities are used by the specialists, others were specific to each field.

- **Academically Gifted**—Children demonstrated traits through role playing and collages. They have also written about examples of good character that they have seen. Each year we choose a charitable organization and collect money. At the close of the school year, a speaker from that charity is invited to come and talk to the children. A check is then presented to the organization.
- **Art**—Students have participated in international art projects. They are now participating in the Iowa Art Project. Pictures will be sent to Iowa where they will represent the rural setting in which we live.

- **Distance Learning Lab**—The Computer Club was formed and be gan making plans to teach computer skills to nursing home residents. They applied for a grant to help with the cost. Many students are corresponding by e-mail to their key pals in other parts of the United States and the world.
- **Educable Mentally Disabled**—The thought for the week and the character trait of the month are displayed in the classroom. When the students made New Year's resolutions, we discussed what resolutions were and how it involves responsibility, self-discipline, and courage to make changes. Each student wrote down his resolutions on sentence strips and placed them in our pocket charts. When the character trait is introduced at the beginning of each month, the students copy the definition as part of their morning work. The class discusses the trait and the definition. The thought for the week is also copied and discussed daily. Students of the week are chosen from those who exhibit one or more positive character traits.
- **Guidance**—The school counseling program integrates character education into its curriculum. The counselors visit classrooms and conduct lessons emphasizing the trait for that month. They also have small group sessions such as an anger management/self-control group that relates to self-discipline, and a friendship skills group that relates to caring and cooperation. We have a "Save One Student" (S.O.S.) program in which a staff member is paired with a student as a supportive friend.
- **Learning Disabled**—Writing All About Me books help students develop self-esteem and self-respect. We discuss how people are different and how they learn differently. We talk about what we can do. Behavior contracts are used to encourage self-discipline. Grades are given on effort and perseverance and achievement.
- **Media Center**—The media specialist uses a game called "Responsible Eggs" to encourage the students. There is a large container that contains plastic eggs that are numbered. The last ten minutes of class, eggs are selected randomly. Students whose numbers are chosen earn free time if they have shown responsibility by caring for and returning library books. Free computer time is given to the Students of the Week. The Media Assistant set up a special character education category on the computer for our materials and assigned a subject heading for these titles.
- **Music**—A collection of all the Thoughts for the Week is displayed in the music room on creative shapes that get the students' attention.

- **Physical Education**—When a student shows good character traits, he is chosen as the Student of the Week and the assistant for the day. Sportsmanship and safety fit in naturally with character education. Using the equipment properly and sharing personal space with others are ways of showing respect. Jump Rope for Heart is a national service project that raises money for the American Heart Association. While participating in this project, children demonstrate perseverance when learning new skills and caring when  helping others accomplish these skills. Group juggling, team workout, and parachute activities are examples of cooperative experiences. In order to win a fitness medal, children accept the responsibility to eat nutritious foods, to exercise three times a week, and to  record their efforts. Students from the fifth grade who exhibit good  character traits are chosen as field day helpers. The gym walls are  decorated with catchy sayings. One of the children's favorites is the  following:

> I may not be the strongest.
> I may not pass each test.
> But when it comes to trying.
> I'll do my very BEST!

- **Spanish**—The character traits are displayed and discussed in Spanish, rather than English.
- **Speech**—Students with exceptional character traits were chosen to go on a special field trip that included going out to dinner.
- **Title I**—We acknowledge our Student of the Week with a special card. This is presented to the student in front of his peers and then he takes the card back to his classroom. The card shows that he is honored that week and also reminds him and his teacher that he is to come to the lobby on Fridays to have his picture taken for the school newspaper.

## Successful Community Involvement Activities

Our **Community Involvement Committee** strives to involve parents by sponsoring parenting workshops, providing needed transportation to school functions and getting reading tutors. Parents are invited to school for many events such as "Muffins for Mom" and "Doughnuts for Dads." Two popular community events are Family Fun Night in October and a tree lighting in December.

The **Parent Resource Center** is set up in the Media Center. Free pamphlets, old teaching materials and parenting tips are available. There are books and videos that can be checked out.

**Business Partners** from various local businesses have supported our Character Education and ACE programs in a variety of ways. They have contributed money and coupons to be used as rewards and incentives. Our Character Education Boxes were donated by one of our business partners.

## Evaluation

The responses to our survey show that our Character Education Program has been a positive, unifying force for our school. We have seen many changes since we began concentrating on character building.

Our personal favorite way of knowing our program is a success is a note written by a fifth grader and handed to our principal. It said: "Here are a few thoughts that I made up that I think would be good to use as thoughts for the week." Clearly the children *are* listening to our message and learning about good character!

Other successes are:

- According to our principal and assistant principal, students are more likely to talk about their problems and are willing to apologize to each other with little or no coaxing from them.
- Most office referrals are for newcomers who have not experienced the concentrated emphasis of our Character Education Program.
- Students show more caring and kindness when trying to get along with each other.
- The children know the character traits and what they mean. These words have become part of their daily vocabulary. Standards of acceptable behavior are clearer.
- When encouraging their students to have positive character traits, teachers are motivated to examine their own actions.
- Students' survey responses show they have more respect for themselves and others, and they also appreciate the diversity in people. Students are able to make wiser decisions about their actions.
- Discipline has improved in the classrooms. Children work hard to be chosen as Student of the Week because they enjoy the special recognition and honor.
- Relationships between students and between teachers and students have improved. Everyone realizes there are no quick fixes to problems, but solutions are systematic and long-term.

- Parents comment that their children seem to fight less with their siblings at home and are more respectful of each others' feelings.
- There is a lot of enthusiasm and a common goal has been set throughout the school.
- Teachers have high expectations for the students and the students are living up to these expectations.

## Future Plans

We plan to continue what we are doing, but we also have a lot of new ideas. Some of them are as follows:
- We'd like to have staff development by Dr. Philip Vincent and also have him as a guest speaker at a PTA meeting.
- We want to involve bus drivers and cafeteria staff by asking them to select outstanding students on the buses and to choose special classes in the cafeteria. The names of these students and classes will be posted.
- Good Character Awards—Each staff member will be given "Good Character Awards" and will be asked to present one each week to students throughout the school who are "caught being good."
- We want to expand our S.O.S. mentoring program.
- We will have an orientation of our character education program for newcomers to our school. This will help new students know what is expected of them.
- We will encourage more staff, parent, and community involvement.
- We will get information about grants that are available to fund materials and activities.
- Every month, a box will be sent around to the classrooms. Each teacher will put in one example of some way he or she is teaching the trait for that month.
- We're planning staff development so we can share successful ideas.
- During Character Education Week, we'll have special daily activities.
- Our Computer Club will apply for a grant to help finance the teaching of Internet skills and e-mail to residents of a local nursing home.
- We plan to have more service projects.
- Our character education scrapbook will be sent around to all the classrooms so that all of the students can see it.

In conclusion, I'd like to offer special thanks to our PTA, which has supported us with our character education emphasis, just as it has always supported our children and teachers in all we do; to our entire staff for all its hard work and for being excellent role models for our next generation. And thanks to a wonderful Character Education Committee that has spent many hours working on our character education program.

Life in our school isn't perfect, and we still have discipline problems, but there's noticeable improvement in behavior and attitude among our students. Rural Hall Elementary is a nicer place to be because students are respectful and caring. Morale among teachers and staff is very high because we can see our students increasingly demonstrating good character, and we know we've made that possible. We're building in these children a strong, positive foundation that will benefit them all their lives.

**For more information or questions about our program, please contact:**
**Mr. Bill Moser**
Health/Character Education Program Specialist
Winston-Salem/Forsyth County Schools
1605 Miller Street
Winston-Salem, NC  27102-2513
(336) 727-8536  Fax (336) 727-2791

# *8* THOMASVILLE, NC

## Successful Character Education at Thomasville Primary School

**Ivan Crissman**
Principal, Thomasville Primary School

During the 1995-1996 school year, we at Thomasville Primary School, in Thomasville, North Carolina, concluded that we needed a schoolwide focus that would unite students, faculty, staff, and administrators. The natural choice was a focus on character education, a choice that has not only united a very large faculty, but also has added new dimensions of order and caring to our student population.

With a staff of over 130 people, Thomasville Primary School serves all the kindergarten through third grade students in the Thomasville community. Including four preschool classes, student population is nearly 1,000. Demographics for the school include a disadvantaged population (as measured by those receiving free and reduced lunches) of almost two-thirds. The Exceptional Children's headcount remains annually higher than 20% of the student population. The school currently has four Educable Mentally Handicapped classes and one Behavioral and Emotional Handicapped class.

The Character Education Program at Thomasville Primary School began on the first teacher workday of the 1996-97 school year. By the end of the second work day teachers were busily engaged in making a plan for schoolwide implementation of character education. Over a three-year period, the program was to include these elements:

- Rules and procedures
- Wise use of good literature in the classroom
- Cooperative learning on a regular basis
- Encouragement of higher level thinking
- Incorporation of service learning into the curriculum

The first order of business was to decide what character traits would become the focus of our program. After much debate, we agreed that we would focus on only three traits—respect, responsibility, and cooperation. With only three traits to teach, we felt not only that the children could easily remember these, but also that it would be much easier to maintain a focus throughout the entire school year. These words are currently found on bulletin boards and in assignments throughout the school. If a child is sent to the office for discipline, he or she will hear at least one of these words. Subsequently, courtesy has been added to the list as an outward expression of the other three traits. These four traits have become known as "RRCC" behavior.

The next order of business was the necessity of schoolwide rules in certain areas of the building, specifically the hallways and the cafeteria. High expectations in these areas set the tone for expectations of behavior throughout the school. Rules were developed in each area by consensus. It was also agreed that if these were important, then we as a faculty would not only spend time teaching these rules, but also practicing them. Students spent many hours at school practicing walking correctly in the halls and in the cafeteria. The message became clear to students that these rules were important and that everyone in the school must follow them.

## Rewarding Positive Behavior

To encourage those classes that did a good job teaching and practicing RRCC behavior, we developed an award system. Award ribbons were cut out of construction paper using the letter-cutting machine and had RRCC printed on them. Initially administrators passed these out to deserving classes in the hallways or cafeteria. In order to provide better coverage for awards and to get students in the habit of watching for other students exhibiting RRCC behavior, award ribbons were given to teachers with the instruction that they could only be given to other classes, never their own. Students often take part in the selection of deserving classes. If a class (in the teacher's judgment) deserves an award and has been overlooked, the teacher is encouraged to let another teacher or an administrator watch for an opportunity to make an appropriate award. Teachers then display these awards in a certain area of their classrooms and use them to set classroom goals and rewards based on the number of awards their class receives. The students have been very responsive to this award system. The awards are only as effective, however, as the teacher allows them to be by the importance she places upon them.

We have found it important to revise the award program periodically to keep the program fresh for the children. Thus for the second year of the program, we changed the award. In the fall we used a leaf to be placed on a bare tree in the classroom, and in the spring the award was a tulip to be placed in a classroom garden. We also added in the final nine weeks of school an RRCC flag. Each class of students with their teacher designed a flag to be displayed daily outside the classroom, but only when the class had earned the right to do so. The teachers and the students determined the criteria for their classroom to be able to display the flag in the hallway. Blank flags and hanging clips were provided for each teacher. Sweeps into each classroom by administrators looking for RRCC behavior are now facilitated by the use of flags outside the door. Periodically award flowers are delivered to each class displaying a flag.

Individual students who regularly display RRCC behavior or who demonstrate a character trait by some specific act are recognized on a weekly schoolwide television broadcast. Students are individually brought before the camera to receive their awards and the reasons for their selections are made known to the entire school. Likewise, the Terrific Kids Program, sponsored by the Kiwanis Club, recognizes individual students, along with their parents, at a monthly breakfast with the principal.

## The Results of Goal Setting

An event we launched during the 1996-97 school year has also helped to foster RRCC principles by requiring students to set goals. With the teacher's assistance, students are asked to set either academic or behavioral goals for the third nine weeks of school. Goals are challenging but realistic. The student and the teacher sign a contract, and a copy is sent home for parents to sign. All the contracts are then posted prominently in the classroom. The teacher is charged with regularly reminding students of their goals and keeping them aware of the time frame.

The reward for successful completion of the goal is participation in a parade through the neighborhood adjoining the school. Community agencies and businesses are solicited for participation, along with secondary school bands and cheerleaders. Those who don't reach their goals are not allowed to participate or watch. Participation rose from 70% the first year to close to 80% the second year. Setting a relatively long-term goal and realizing the responsibility to meet the goal is a new experience for many of these students. (As an aside and to involve parents to a greater degree, parents of students achieving goals are asked to contribute a dollar to the school to be given to a worthy cause in honor of their child's success. This year the money collected went to a school damaged by tornadoes in a nearby community. This event not only taught students valuable character lessons, but also served as an excellent public relations tool.)

## Other Supporting Ideas

During the first year of implementation, our staff chose to include the wise use of character-related literature as a priority. While adopting a new reading series facilitated progress in this area, virtually any literature can be examined in light of moral issues presented by the author. Teachers have become accustomed to looking for character illustrations in all aspects of the curriculum. A current wall display in one of our hallways asks: "Did Peter Rabbit Show RRCC?" Below are the children's pictures and their written responses to the question. To show administrative support and to provide a resource to teachers, a copy of William Bennett's *The Children's Book of Virtues* was provided for each classroom. Supplementing the reading series are videos that stress individual character traits.

At the same time, we began to emphasize service learning. Both classes and grade levels chose projects that reached out from the school into the community and beyond. Examples of projects include:
- Cards and cookies sent to children at the Baptist Children's Home
- School supplies sent to a school damaged by a hurricane
- Blank Christmas cards sent to foreign military bases for use by soldiers
- Fundraising to purchase certain clothes closet items

- Fundraising for flood victims in Kentucky
- Food collection for the Salvation Army
- Adoption and visiting of grandparents at local nursing homes
- Singing Christmas carols at nursing homes
- Fundraising for St. Jude's Children's Hospital
- Fundraising for Cynthia's Kids (a local Christmas fund)
- Sending Valentines to patients in a nearby veteran's hospital
- Periodically picking up trash in the area surrounding the school

Teachers found these projects to be fulfilling and were easily able to use them to stimulate written and verbal interaction in the areas of character. Though service learning has become a requirement of classrooms, I doubt that any teacher would now leave it out of their curriculum.

Through a grant written in conjunction with the University of North Carolina at Greensboro, a fourth area of our character development program has been addressed this school year. So far, twenty-three of our teachers have been trained in the use of cognitively guided instruction in mathematics. This problem-solving approach to teaching math has not only improved students' numerical thinking, but also has improved their overall thinking skills. There is a willingness of many students to now go beyond surface responses to situations that they face daily. This summer the teachers who are currently trained will take further instruction in order to train our entire faculty in the use of Cognitively Guided Instruction.

The final piece of the puzzle, the use of cooperative learning, was already being used in most classrooms, and most teachers have had training in this area. We held a mid-year in-service program to review salient points and different approaches to grouping and evaluation to encourage teachers to incorporate this skill regularly into their lesson plans. We will do further work in this area in the third year of implementation.

## What Are the Results?

Two years into our Character Education Program, what results can be seen? We now have in our school a marked sense of order among students and staff. Students coming into the building in the morning start their day with an expectation of order in the hallways. They are greeted by staff and reminded of the hall procedures. Staff posted throughout the building monitor, but seldom have to correct students. Students are practicing what they've been taught all year. Likewise, during the day, student movement in the hall is orderly and quiet. When a class occasionally does not meet expectations, the teacher returns the class to the room to try the procedure once more. Dismissal is also quite orderly. Students are dismissed by grade levels and proceed in lines with the teacher to their appropriate dismissal points. It is amazing to stand in the center of the building where all 1,000 students must pass on their way to their pick-up points and to watch the quiet and orderly manner in which they proceed.

The cafeteria is equally as orderly. Students go through the serving lines, where they serve themselves, following procedures taught them all year long. They're not allowed to return to the line to get things later. Talk at the tables is at a minimal vocal level and only to those close by. At most times during the lunch period we have at least ten classes in the cafeteria at one time, but I eat in there most days and can carry on a conversation with anyone around me using a normal conversational tone.

Visitors coming into the building comment on the warm and calm atmosphere. We have many substitute teachers who will not substitute anywhere else. Those who have been coming in and out of the building for a number of years have noted the positive change since character cducation has begun.

Early in the year interns from the University of North Carolina at Greensboro visited with us for a day. Their experience up to that point had been in schools in another system closer to the university. They were so impressed by the atmosphere at Thomasville Primary School that six of them, with the permission of the university, made transportation arrangements to spend part of their second semester internship with us. I talked with them recently, and all of them want to have their student teaching experience at this school.

Interns coming from Thomasville High School feel equally as strongly about what is happening at this school. Communities in Schools volunteers speak glowingly to others within the community of the warmth they feel in our building. A recent survey of parents with over 300 respondents showed a score of 3.74 (on a 4-point scale) on the question of whether ours was an orderly school. When asked if their children liked Thomasville Primary School, they responded with a result of 3.73. The overall grade for the school was 3.69.

Discipline throughout the school has improved notably. Office referrals during the first year of implementation and continuing this year have decreased by approximately one-half. Part of this drop, however, must be attributed to the addition of a Behavioral and Emotionally Handicapped class that was added during our first year of character education. This class serves a maximum of eight students. Students who are sent to the office more easily understand the reasons they were sent and more readily accept responsibility for their actions.

What about test scores? Last year Thomasville Primary School reached exemplary status on statewide end-of-grade tests, indicating a growth rate for our third grade students at least 10% beyond what was expected by the state. While all of the academic growth cannot be attributed to the character education program, certainly a portion of it can. Other factors that contributed to academic success were an after-school tutorial program for at-risk third graders, a schoolwide emphasis on the Accelerated Reader (a computer-based comprehension tester), and the Title I Reading Assistance Program. In addition, Thomasville Primary School is fortunate to have a number of faculty and staff who pray for our school on a regular basis.

## The Teachers' Response

Teachers were initially skeptical about whether the program would make any difference, thinking it might be just another passing fad in education. It didn't take long, however, until they noticed a real difference, especially in students' interaction with teachers and with each other. During the first year of implementation, a class character rating scale was filled out by each teacher two weeks after school started and again at the end of the school year. This questionnaire allowed the teacher to rate her class in fifteen different character areas. Without exception, every score at every grade level showed improvement over the school year. Most notable improvements were in grade one with the overall score rising 36 percent and in grade two with a 27 percent rise. At the end of the second school year of our character education program, the questionnaire was readministered to first, second and third grade teachers to see if there was any cumulative effect for those students who had been involved in the program for two years. They showed that while there was no additional gain after a second year of character education, the increases that were made during the first year were maintained at the same level during the second year.

There is no doubt that character education has made a difference at Thomasville Primary School. We wouldn't dare go back now!

### THOMASVILLE PRIMARY SCHOOL PARENT SURVEY

Please indicate the grade you would give our school in the following areas. Do not give your grade based solely on your experience with one person at the school, but based upon your generall observations. Use A, B, C, D, or F.

\_\_\_ 1. Thomasville Primary tries to meet the academic needs of students.

\_\_\_ 2. Thomasville Primary tries to meet the social/emotional need of its students.

\_\_\_ 3. Thomasville primary treats all students fairly.

\_\_\_ 4. Thomasville Primary is a friendly school.

\_\_\_ 5. Thomasville Primary is an orderly school.

\_\_\_ 6. I feel my child is safe while at Thomasville Primary.

\_\_\_ 7. As a parent, I feel welcome at Thomasville Primary.

\_\_\_ 8. My child likes Thomasville Primary School.

\_\_\_ 9. My overall grade for Thomasville Primary School.

How long have you been associated with Thomasville Primary School?

_____

Please use the space below to make any comments or suggestions that will help us to plan the future of Thomasville Primary School.

## THOMASVILLE PRIMARY SCHOOL TEACHER SURVEY

Name_____

Please put a number in the blank by each question to indicate the degree to which you agree with each statement. A 4 indicates you are in total agreement with the statement; a 3 or 2 indicate lower levels of agreement. A 1 indicates you do not agree at all.

____ 1. My students try to resolve problems peacefully.
____ 2. Being honest is important to my students.
____ 3. My students understand about the consequences of poor choices.
____ 4. Doing their best is important to my students.
____ 5. My students treat adults with respect.
____ 6. My students are willing to share with others in the class.
____ 7. Telling the truth is important to my students.
____ 8. My students are willing to take responsibility for their actions.
____ 9. My students are able to set realistic goals for themselves.
____ 10. My students make an effort to treat others in a kind, courteous manner.
____ 11. Cooperation is important to my students.
____ 12. My students respect the differences in others.
____ 13. Helping others is important to my students.
____ 14. My students try to obey school and classroom rules.
____ 15. My students are willing to take a risk to do the right thing.

# 9 DALLAS, TX

---

## A Home-Grown Program

### Dr. Gail Hartin
Principal, University Park Elementary School

University Park Elementary School, located in the Highland Park Independent School District in Dallas, Texas, has about 700 students in grade K-4. The district serves the neighboring cities of Highland Park and University Park and has a total student enrollment of approximately 5,500. This is a close-knit community in which neighborhood schools serve as the focal point for family involvement. Parents play an active role in the schools as volunteers. Approximately 96% of the school system's graduates attend college. Many eventually return to the community to raise their own families.

In 1994, mutual concerns on the part of parents, school staff, and community members were brought to the forefront. These concerns had as their common denominator a lack of empathy on the part of students, as well as their growing inability to "draw the line." This was manifested in student behavior at athletic events and other extracurricular activities, as well as in the increase in frequency and seriousness of "senior pranks." These incidents included racial and sexist innuendoes, with alcohol use in some cases. At the elementary level, there was a growing concern over lack of common courtesy among the students, even in the presence of their parents at school events.

A commitment to a shared solution was evident among the district's administrative team and site-based leadership groups. We all recognized at the outset that involving parents and seeking their support would be a critical component of the improvement process.

Our initial step at University Park involved a discussion in the Campus Leadership Council, a group which includes parent, community, and staff representatives. This group, called the CLC, is co-chaired by the principal and a teacher. The main concerns at the elementary level were identified, and we recognized that these same issues were the basis of more serious misbehavior as the children became older. This same discussion took place in a meeting of the grade level team leaders, which the superintendent and I attended. The same concerns were identified. Several teachers expressed an initial interest in an approach with monthly themes.

The next step was a review of literature conducted by the principal and the team leaders. Numerous articles and books about character development were read and discussed by this group throughout the 1994-95 school year, and a summary was presented to the faculty and the parents. In addition, the principal and other staff members attended workshops on character development to learn about existing programs, particularly those with themes reinforced through the use of literature.

Based on information compiled from the readings and professional workshops, the leadership team concluded that the most productive approach would be to develop a program specifically tailored to University Park's needs, and to integrate it into the culture of the school. One of the team leaders, Mary Goodloe, had seen a broadcast about a school that had set up monthly character themes and had built its own program around them. In April 1995, she sent me a note describing the broadcast and expressing enthusiasm and encouragement about the direction in which University Park was moving. Mrs. Goodloe's tragic drowning death in a May 1995 storm strengthened the faculty's commitment to this effort.

The logical choice for our themes, and our consensus decision, was the school's ten core values, which had been adopted by the Campus Leadership Council in 1993. These were: Excellence, Commitment, Cooperation, Communication, Caring, Respect, Integrity, Inspiration, Growth and Celebration. Since these core values were the result of a consensus-building process and were already a part of the school culture, it made good sense to build on them. They were already posted in every classroom. Posters with inspirational messages relating to the core values were purchased and displayed throughout the school.

Other strengths already in place included a strong language arts program and a staff well informed in cooperative learning, teaching thinking skills, and service learning. Furthermore, a cross-grade-level "buddy program" was in place, and the school had already begun to move away from a reward/punishment model of discipline and was focused on a more proactive approach intended to build self-discipline and responsibility by teaching pro-social behavior. In addition to the state-mandated Code of Conduct, students received a list of schoolwide expectations stated in simple, positive, "kid-friendly" language. This list was known as the Panther Code of Conduct, in honor of the school's mascot.

In order to build on these strengths and to cement them into a cohesive framework, staff development sessions on character, conflict resolution, and communication skills were offered at the beginning of the 1995-96 school year. Each staff member was given a copy of Stephen Covey's book, *The 7 Habits of Highly Effective People*, to read over the summer in preparation for this. Because the group's research had shown that modeling is an essential part of character development, Covey's book was used as a point of departure to help teachers set goals to be powerful role models.

At an orientation presentation for staff members, the concept of monthly themes was presented to the staff. The plan was that at first, the themes would be introduced through weekly letters from the principal to the students. Within each monthly theme, related themes were developed for each week. These formed the basis for each weekly letter. For example, February's overall theme, integrity, included the ideas of honesty, fairness, trust, trustworthiness and courage.

The next step was to have school counselor Billie Kissinger integrate the themes into her classroom guidance lessons, which are conducted in the classroom with the teacher present. Finally, teachers would be encouraged to work the themes into their lessons and into their disciplinary interactions with students. In this way, teachers would regard character development not as something to add on, but rather as something to weave in. Sometimes students decided to respond to the principal's letter, or to create a banner, poem or skit about the theme. Other times, natural connections occurred, such as the connection with the theme of commitment during a unit on immigration in the fourth grade.

Each grade level already had a particular service learning project. These were reviewed to ensure that they were projects which were truly meaningful to the children. A parent volunteer was asked to coordinate all of the projects and to serve as a contact person with community agencies who would be the beneficiaries. Among the beneficiaries are Children's Medical Center, Scottish Rite Hospital, the North Texas Food Bank, and a number of social service agencies. A team of six staff members and one parent attended training for the CHAMPS Peer Leadership Program, and the program was implemented in the fourth grade. Examples of CHAMPS projects include making morning announcements related to the monthly character themes, helping in the clinic and library, and conducting schoolwide projects to promote school spirit, safety and environmental awareness.

Parent education was seen as a key component of University Park's character development goal. Parent workshops with guest speakers were held in the evenings. Topics included: How to talk so kids will listen and how to listen so kids will talk; and How to raise a dependable, capable, responsible child. Each monthly school newsletter contained articles about character development written by the principal, counselor or PTA officers.

## Evaluating Our Efforts

At the end of the 1995-96 school year, we conducted an evaluation. Using Dr. Vincent's "five elements of character development" as a rubric, three goals were identified. Responses to faculty questionnaires confirmed a strong feeling among teachers that strengthening character development needed to take priority over vertical teaming in the academic disciplines. Teacher comments indicated that this was an important foundation upon which academic excellence could be built. The first goal was a more formalized framework for integrating character development into teaching literature. The second was continued refinement of our efforts to promote prosocial student behavior. The third was to promote age-appropriate levels of responsibility and independence in the students.

A staff retreat was held in July 1996 to kick off these efforts. Each staff member received a copy of Positive Discipline in the Classroom to read in preparation. The retreat speaker was Madelyn Swift, author of *Discipline for Life*. At the retreat, teachers were asked to recommit to cooperative learning as a bridge to the use of class meetings. The use of T-charts to show what character traits and their related social skills look like and sound like was modeled and encouraged. Each grade level was asked to review an extensive list of children's literature which had been indexed by character themes, and to identify the works which were part of the curriculum for their respective grade level.

During the 1996-97 school year, teachers incorporated the use of class meetings. The principal and the counselor also used class meetings when dealing with most disciplinary and social issues. This was a significant milestone in the paradigm shift from discipline as something that is done to students to something that is taught to students.

A schoolwide attention signal was implemented and taught to all classes. Posters defining voice levels ranging from zero (silence) to 5 (heard across the room) were posted in each room.

Additional resources, such as videos, posters and puppets, were purchased for the counselor to use in her classroom guidance lessons. New materials, such as Dr. Thomas Lickona's video, "Character Education," were added to the professional library as well.

Media Specialist Tyna Adams created a monthly list of literature related to that month's theme. A display was also set up in the Media Center highlighting some of the monthly selections. When the school purchased the Accelerated Reader program, a computer program which allows students to test their comprehension and track their progress, the media specialist wrote tests to accompany some of the principal's weekly letters.

Vertical teams within the school worked on a continuum of levels of responsibility by grade level. The Campus Leadership Council endorsed this list and named it "A Panther's Guide to Responsibility." It took nearly the entire school year to finalize the list, which was presented to parents as part of each teacher's presentation at Open House in August.

Ernest Boyer's *The Basic School: A Community for Learning* became the subject of study and discussion for the Campus Leadership council. Its four priorities (the school as a community, a curriculum with coherence, a climate for learning, and a commitment to character) evolved into a framework for self-evaluation and improvement planning.

In November 1996, University Park received the Diamond Shamrock "Hooray for Excellence" Award for a tape prepared by Dr. Hartin, music teacher Karen Zukoski, and a group of third graders. The tape described the school's character development program.

In November, Dr. Vincent visited the Highland Park Independent School District and spent time on each campus. During the visit to University Park, it became apparent that of his five elements of character education, the element related to teaching for thinking was still unclear to the faculty. After Dr. Vincent's visit, team leaders at University Park set about establishing a consistent set of graphic organizers for vertical use. Teachers submitted their own favorite graphic organizers, and a varied set was compiled.

The staff expressed an interest in learning more about emotional intelligence as a backdrop for character development. Articles, books and videos on this topic were made available to staff and parents. Continuing education opportunities on emotional intelligence were offered through the principal's parent coffees and faculty study groups.

## More Feedback and Evaluation

Each year, a short survey is sent to parents with the January report card. Parents have the opportunity to offer comments about things which they particularly like, along with any concerns, questions, or requests for further information. The response rate is generally 90% or higher. Teachers and the principal review each survey, and individual responses are made by the homeroom teacher, or, if appropriate, by the principal. Survey results are reviewed by the Campus Leadership Council for any recurring patterns. One such pattern in both the 1996 and 1997 surveys was positive comments about our efforts to teach respect, manners and self-discipline.

In March 1997, the Campus Leadership Council met to begin formulating goals for the 1997-98 school year. Echoing concerns voiced by parents, the CLC expressed concern that our character development efforts wouldn't take root if we did not address fundamental issues like hallway safety and lunchroom etiquette. School procedures, which had worked effectively for a student body of 500, did not work well with 700 students. This was compounded by our use of numerous portable buildings on the campus. Furthermore, traffic congestion had increased exponentially trying to access a landlocked campus with no bus transportation.

In April, the Campus Leadership Council met with Dr. Vincent again. He was asked to talk about rules and procedures, since they form the hub of his character development model. Based on the insights gained during his visit, a subcommittee of volunteers from the CLC, under the leadership of co-chair Dr. Greg Granath, drafted a revised set of school procedures. This comprehensive plan included procedures for arrival and dismissal, hallways, recess, lunch, assemblies, and restrooms. Procedures such as the school signal and 0-5 voice levels were incorporated.

The proposal included total faculty involvement, with teachers sharing responsibility for morning greeting (a more positive way of viewing morning supervision) and for accompanying their classes to designated exits at the end of the day. Responsibilities of students, teachers and parents were clearly stated. It was also emphasized that, in keeping with what the staff had learned in the course of studying *The 7 Habits*, colleagues would be expected to give each other honest, direct feedback throughout the implementation process. The expectation was set that teachers would use class meetings as a problem-solving tool for classes needing support in successfully following school procedures. Just as a lack of academic success signals a need for re-teaching, so also a lack of success with procedures indicates a need for re-teaching. The proposal was unanimously approved by the Campus Leadership Council, and the subcommittee prepared to present it at the opening staff development in August.

At the end of the 1996-97 school year, each team or department completed an evaluation of the progress toward the three goals identified for the year. The feedback obtained was complimentary of the individual components such as the principal's letters, CHAMPS projects, literature displays, Panther's Guide to Responsibility, etc. The main suggestion was that the goal of improving school procedures be earnestly addressed from the moment school started in August.

## Making It Real

In preparation for the 1997-98 year, the principal gave each faculty member a copy of *The Basic School* to read during the summer. The opening staff development was presented in the context of the four priorities outlined by Ernest Boyer. Meanwhile, Dr. Hartin and the PTA worked with the City of University Park to make changes in the traffic pattern around the school to ensure greater safety at dismissal. Instructions for parents were posted prior to the opening of school. Despite complaints from parents that the new dismissal plan created personal inconvenience for them, it was implemented the first day of school and has remained in effect.

Teachers presented the new procedures to students the first week of school in the context of the monthly theme of Excellence. The principal and counselors visited each classroom to talk about quality and caring. The school procedures and the "Panther's Guide to Responsibility" were reviewed with parents at Open House during the second week of school.

Monthly progress reports were given at staff meetings and CLC meetings. In January 1998, teachers completed a "Mid-year Reflection" form and participated in a discussion which resulted in some fine-tuning of arrival and dismissal procedures. The most meaningful feedback came when one of University Park's retired teachers was substitute teaching in December and commented on what an improvement she noticed over the previous year.

Recognizing that our experiences might help other schools with similar goals, we have sought out opportunities to share ideas with others. Presentations have been given by the principal, counselors and teachers at administrative retreats, at new teacher orientation, local staff development workshops, state and national conferences, and parent meetings. With the help of the high school's broadcasting class, a videotape about character education at University Park was prepared for use in workshops, parent meetings and school tours.

## Support from the School District

One of the most inspiring forces was the support of Superintendent John Connolly and the Board of Trustees. Dr. Connolly made character development the focus of his convocation address in 1995 and served as a co-presenter with principals Gail Hartin and Jane Robbins at a state conference in 1996.

The Board of Trustees identified character development as a priority to be addressed in the district's strategic plan. Director of Instruction Linda Salinas created a Character Development Task Force to provide a shared framework for addressing character education. A Systems Alignment Project, initiated this school year by Assistant Superintendent Jean Rutherford, now has as part of its focus the integration of character development into every academic discipline and into every aspect of the school system, including recruitment and hiring.

Has all this made a difference? As I reflect on how different the school looks now from the way it looked five years ago, the words that come to mind are responsibility, respect, reflection and renewal. Discipline referrals have decreased significantly because teachers are teaching conflict resolution strategies and using class meetings to address many day-to-day issues. When students are referred, there is no longer an expectation that the question will be, "What do we need to do to this student?" but rather, "What do we need to teach this student, and how can we best accomplish this?"

Students now are accepting greater responsibility for their work, for their actions, and for solving school problems. Both students and teachers display greater sensitivity to the big picture. Demonstrations of leadership by teachers has increased tenfold. All in all, the issue of character development have created a heightened sense of "one-ness" among students, faculty, parents, and community.

# 10 WINSTON-SALEM, NC

## Character in Practice
## at Vienna Elementary School

**Debbie S. Woodson**
Counselor, Vienna Elementary School

Vienna Elementary School, located in the western part of Forsyth County near Winston-Salem, North Carolina, is a K-5 school with 661 students and 67 staff members. Vienna is a communication-themed school, and integration of communication skills throughout the curriculum is emphasized. The specialists (media, music, visual art, physical education, and guidance) use multi-sensory approaches to have the students recognize the various ways of communicating. We practice conflict mediation. Vienna's mission is to have all students become responsible citizens, as well as academically proficient and productive workers in our changing society. Pat Compton, our principal, has always promoted high academic standards and good manners in our school.

In 1995, the Winston-Salem/Forsyth County school system set up a committee to study character education. It was composed of religious leaders, businessmen/women, school administrators, parents, and teachers, who all spent many hours in research and discussion to determine which character traits should be emphasized. After they reached consensus, the superintendent and school board decided that character education would be implemented beginning in the 1996-97 school year. The seven traits to be emphasized were:

**RESPONSIBILITY** Being dependable by carrying out duties and obligations.

**RESPECT** Recognizing and accepting your inherent worth and according that same worth and value to others.

**SELF-DISCIPLINE** Demonstrating hard work and commitment to purpose.

**CARING** Being considerate, courteous, helpful, kind, sensitive to and understanding of others—regardless of race, age, gender or religion.

**INTEGRITY** Having the inner strength to be truthful, tustwrorthy, honest and dependable in all things.

**PERSEVERANCE** Being persistent in pursuit of worthy objectives in spite of difficult opposition or discouragement.

**COURAGE** Having the internal determination to act according to the principles of good character even when others don't.

## Implementation Ideas by Grade Level

Vienna integrated the character education traits into its School Improvement Plan and schoolwide curriculum. Following are some activities and strategies used to implement character education at our school.

At the **kindergarten** level, each child is encouraged to take responsibility for his or her own actions. Positive behaviors are recognized, and children are taught alternative ways to solve problems. Songs, stories, audio and visual aids are used to reinforce lessons about the selected character traits. Students are recognized as "Student of the Week," "Super Star Student" or "Child of the Day." All recognitions emphasize various character traits and are highlighted when referring to the honored student. A bulletin board is decorated with special items that the student might want to share.

Students in **first grade** also have a "Student of the Week" board. They bring in pictures, favorite items and/or interesting information about themselves. An information sheet is completed by the students that includes character traits they believe they possess. Class meetings are often held to discuss classroom issues such as behavior expectations.

Making good choices and positive ways to resolve problems are also discussed during class meetings. These meetings are often used as avenues to share "good things" about children in the class. Character traits are included in as many areas as possible. When the first grade team did its Colonial Day celebration, for example, much emphasis was placed on comparing life styles of today with those of yesterday and deciding what character traits and values were demonstrated during the Colonial Days.

All of our classrooms have posters with the character traits written on them, but those in the **second grade** rooms immediately get your attention. Some of the posters are fashioned after a caterpillar, and some have pictures of children demonstrating the character traits. Others show a giant ice cream cone with the character traits written on different flavors of ice cream, or a lion-themed bulletin board titled "Roaring About Good Friends" with positive traits observed by friends in the class. The second graders enjoy recognizing the student of the week. Each student is asked to use a card and write about the honored student describing character traits that he or she exhibits. The cards are then collected, made into a booklet and given to the honored student to share with family and friends.

Words unique to the character education program are included in the weekly spelling assignment and the character traits are sought in all literature experiences (reading series and media materials). Students are encouraged to write their own stories that depict character traits, and the following is a story written by one of our second graders.

### Friends

Once upon a time Kyle was my best friend. Then Michael, Andrew and Kyle began to play together. I felt left out. But I began to go on with my life. After a few months, that is when I started to be mean. I just couldn't go it without my friend Kyle. Kyle taught me everything I knew so well. A few months later some other boys became my friends. Well, they made me laugh in class and I started getting in trouble all the time. I kept getting sadder and sadder. Then one day Kyle picked me for deputy. We had a talk about our friendship. Then Andrew, Michael, Kyle and I started our own club. We got a club named "Character Traits." We use traits like perseverance, responsibility, respect, courage, caring, integrity and self-discipline. Now we ride our bikes together. We shoot basketball. We run together in the gym. I have learned that you can't choose one or the other. It's best to have good friends.

The **third grade** classes work hard to reinforce the character traits by teaching the children to work in cooperative learning groups. By doing so, students learn to listen to each other, cooperate and respect one another. All these concepts are stressed, modeled and practiced until they become a natural part of the daily routines. During some of the language arts classes, stories are written about famous people. Books such as *Miss Nelson Is Missing*, *John Henry*, and *The Three Little Pigs* are read, and character traits are recognized and outlined. A slogan in one of the third grade classrooms summarizes what character education is all about: "It's nice to be important, but it's more important to be nice!"

One character trait is emphasized each month in the **fourth grade** classes. Role playing, story sharing, booklet making, and class discussions are some of the strategies that fourth grades use in their classes. Special guests are invited to share stories that capture the interest of the students and to help the children understand and appreciate cultural diversity. An African collection, borrowed from Winston-Salem State University, contains authentic instruments, pictures, carvings, and lesson plans for use in many diverse activities. (All teachers participated in a workshop on African-American Culture which is a part of the Afro-American Infusion Project for our school system. The workshop was led by Dr. Stewart, a professor from Wake Forest University. She shared with us many literature books that could be infused into the Standard Course of Study and Character Education.) Children write and learn about African-American culture, as well as other cultures throughout the year which encourages respect for ethnic differences.

One of the ways that the **fifth grade** classes incorporate the seven character traits into their curriculum is by engaging in a program called "Learning for Life," developed by the Boy Scouts of America. This program emphasizes positive values and helps to develop positive social skills and enhances self-esteem. At the end of the year, the fifth grade students, along with their teachers and parents, take a field trip to Raven's Knob (a Boy Scout camp) where the various skills that have been taught in class are practiced and applied. In the reading series, the character traits are identified in each story. Students discuss how the story characters depict certain traits. Cooperative learning and working with partners are exercised to help the children in assisting and supporting each other in their classes.

# Special Programs by Specialists

Our specialists do a wonderful job of integrating character education into their curriculums. They, too, have the character traits posted in their areas and reinforce the slogans of the week on a daily basis.

Our **media specialist** reads stories, shows videos, and discusses the different character traits with the children. They hear stories about how kindness prevails, as realized in the story *Mufosoe's Beautiful Daughter*, and/or how honesty is the best policy, as in *The Boy Who Cried Wolf*.

Character education is brought to life in living color as our **art teacher** shares with the children her talent and appreciation for a variety of art media and cultural art pieces. Art from various cultures are examined, worked on, and displayed for all to admire and learn from.

The **French teacher** compares values and character traits of the French culture with American cultures. Children in kindergarten through fifth grade learn how important good manners are to the French culture. A young gentleman from France came to speak to some of the French classes to share first-hand experiences related to French culture.

Our Core I and II **Exceptional classes** participate in the "Slogan of the Week" program, and their teachers are constantly reinforcing and practicing the character traits. They engage in role-playing with the children and invite special guests to visit and share with the classes. One guest speaker elaborated on the care, respect, and appreciation of animals. Snakes, lizards, and other pets were brought in for the children to view. The children were allowed to touch some of the animals.

Our **Learning Disabilities teacher** works in small groups and reinforces the character traits through the reading series, writing, and other areas of instruction. Students taking speech must be responsible for their speech folders and monitor their progress. Perseverance and self-corrections are stressed, and progress is depicted on visual charts.

The **Academically Gifted teacher** challenges her students to bring in newspaper articles about individuals who demonstrate the selected character traits. These current events are discussed and shared with other members of the class.

Our **Curriculum Coordinator** works closely with teachers to help them serve the students more effectively. She also helps individual students to build self-esteem and confidence by helping them to experience success.

We do have some students who need time out of the regular class for short periods. Our **"Time Out" Coordinator** not only monitors these children but he also tutors and talks with them about alternative choices. These alternative choices often require character adjustments on the part of the students.

# Schoolwide Programs

In addition to these class activities on character education, our students participate in schoolwide activities dealing with character.

The Work Buddies Program and The Character Education Recognition Program were initiated by our assistant principal, Teresa Dees. This program matches some students with faculty and staff in an effort to provide some opportunities for those students to work with adults and share special times with them. The students spend thirty to forty-five minutes helping the adults to complete a variety of jobs (running errands, operating the copier, and/or stacking items in the supply closet). The adult gives encouragement and serves as a positive role model. It is believed that this program also helps our children become givers in society rather than takers.

In the Character Education Recognition Program, anyone in the school may observe and recognize a student who has demonstrated one or more of the character traits. The observer completes a form by writing the child's name, grade and teacher on it and a brief description of the trait observed. The form is sent to the assistant principal and the student is recognized over the public address system and is awarded a certificate. A letter is also sent to the parent(s) informing them of their child's accomplishments. Students who are recognized are randomly selected from each grade level to have lunch with the assistant principal at the end of the week. This program has been very successful. Students are now recognizing and praising their teachers and other school personnel. Friends are recognizing friends, and siblings are recognizing each other.

Jog for Character is an exercise program that was implemented by our physical education and health teacher, Mrs. Nancy Hoover. As in any type of exercise program, this program, too, requires self-discipline and dedication. The students and their teachers jog or walk at least one mile a week. After a mile is completed, the class and their teacher are recognized schoolwide. (The first five miles represent honesty, the second five miles represent responsibility, the third five miles represent courage, the fourth five miles represent perseverance). Jog for Character posters are hung on the outside of the classroom door displaying the level of accomplishments. Some teachers have elected to participate in this program on an individual basis. It is a great program that helps the participants stay healthy and fit.

Our student council is very active and sponsors a variety of events throughout the year. The Council is composed of representatives from each class in grades three, four, and five, and the Core II class. Some of the activities sponsored by the student council are the Canned Food Drive, Toy Drive, Samaritan Soup Kitchen Penny Campaign, and Skate Night. Students, teachers, and parents donate food to the local soup kitchen and to needy families in our school. Used toys are collected and donated to needy families. Collections from the Penny Campaign are given to the Samaritan Soup Kitchen. Money is also raised by the Student Council by sponsoring skate parties at the local skating rink. Some of this money has been used to beautify the school's court yard, to purchase a memorial plaque for a health room worker who passed away in 1997, and to fill "goodie bags" for teachers and staff on holidays and during Teacher Appreciation Week. The council has also contributed books and videos to our media center and made contributions to Brenner Children's Hospital.

# National Character Education Week

During National Character Education Week, which is held the third week in October, special activities are held for the entire school. Kathryn Seni, a former counseling intern, along with the Character Education Committee, coordinated the activities for a successful "Character Education Week." During that week in 1997, Vienna participated in a number of activities and events that highlighted the importance of exhibiting good character. Different themes were highlighted each day. Monday was giving and sharing day; Tuesday was positive attitude and self-discipline day; Wednesday was good manners day; Thursday was environmental awareness day; and Friday was happy day. During this week, guest speakers were featured on our "Tiger TV" through our TV production studio. Some of the people and places featured were Sonya Kurosky, director of the Samaritan Soup Kitchen; Dr. Donald Martin, superintendent of our school system; Area Superintendent Toni Bigham; Bill Moser, Program Specialist for Character Education and Health; Charlie Davis, Assistant Athletic Director for Wake Forest University; Dr. Paul Orser, Associate Dean for Freshmen at Wake Forest University; Officer Chris Lawson,

DARE Officer; Yvette Evans, director of Keep Winston-Salem Beautiful; Brooke Anderson, Curator of Diggs Gallery at Winston-Salem State University; and Mrs. Geraldine Davis, representing the Delta Fine Arts Center.

Each grade level had a guest speaker that visited and discussed such topics as recycling, keeping the environment clean, pet owner responsibilities, appreciation for cultural differences, and safety. Storytellers, whose stories featured those character traits related to our character education program, also visited. During this special week McGruff, the Crime Dog (who was really Freddie Holland, our custodian) and Barkly B. Green, a huge tree (who was really Rex Brewer, fiancé of Kathryn Seni), greeted the students in the lobby. These characters were popular with the children.

Character scrapbooks were made in classrooms and displayed for everyone to see. On the outside of classroom doors were original slogans that classes had chosen to be their slogan for the entire year. It was during this week that the Student Council kicked off its annual Food Drive and Penny Campaign. This week proved to be a rewarding experience for everyone and all children were issued "Certificates of Appreciation" for participating in the Character Education Celebration.

## The Guidance Program Contribution

The Guidance Department plays a vital role in the school's character education program. The Guidance Counselor disseminates information to the staff sent from the school system's character education specialist and re-emphasizes character education in her classroom guidance classes. Mrs. Woodson, our counselor, teaches lessons that also include multi-sensory approaches. Children have opportunities to role-play, sing, dance, draw, write, read, and work in small groups. Some of the songs that the children sing contain her original lyrics sung to familiar tunes:

Helpful, Helpful Little Child (tune: *Twinkle, Twinkle Little Star*)
Showing me your lovely smile.
Being friendly, being kind.
Think good thoughts within your mind,
Helpful, Helpful Little Child,
Showing me your lovely smile.

I am honest (tune: *Are You Sleeping?*)
I am honest,
Yes I am, Yes I am,
An honest little boy,
An honest little girl,
That is me, That is me.

The slogan of the week program was initiated by our guidance teacher. A new slogan is announced every week and displayed in the classrooms. Students are asked to recite the slogan of the week in guidance classes to reinforce its meaning. Children often come in to guidance class asking to recite the slogan of the week.

Character education has proven to be an asset to our school and our students. The climate of the school is warm and caring. It is so noticeable that visitors comment on how friendly the people are at Vienna. The adults care about the students, and they care about each other. They provide a child-centered atmosphere with rules that are fair and systems that allow students to make choices. The adults at Vienna are excellent role models for character. In all aspects of our school, everyone encourages, reinforces, models, and compliments students in regard to their behaviors. Students seem to have internalized positive character traits. In 1997, our school was cited as a "School of Distinction" by the North Carolina Department of Public Instruction.

# 11 HIGH POINT, NC

## Making a Big Impact with Small Classroom Habits

**Charlie Abourjilie**
Southwest High School
High Point, NC

One day in September 1983, I decided I wanted to be a high school teacher. I was in my first few weeks of community college in Richmond, Virginia, and my history professor changed my life. Professor James O'Brian made learning so enjoyable that I knew that was what I wanted to do with high school students. I had some very nice teachers in high school, but none really motivated me or pushed me to do more with my life. I was a nice kid and very average student. I probably could have fallen through the cracks and ended up going nowhere. I was never encouraged to go to college or take the tougher classes.

In the spring of my senior year, many of my friends were getting acceptances to colleges and universities but I wasn't. Community college was the highest I could reach at that time. But it was there this wonderful professor awakened in me the love of learning. I came to love learning so much I knew I wanted to try to instill that in young people as my life's work. I wanted to make a difference in the lives of kids that might otherwise fall through the cracks—kids like I had been.

I studied like I had never studied in high school, and from community college, I went on to get an Education Social Studies degree at Virginia Polytechnic Institute and State University. I earned my teacher's certification in secondary education and began teaching social studies at what was then called Southwest Guilford High School in High Point, N.C. In the eleven years since then, I have learned a thing or two from great teachers I've taught with or heard speak. As Harry Wong says, I try to "beg, borrow, and steal" from the very best. Educators such as Harry Wong, Marva Collins, Clare Lameres, Hal Urban, Tom Lickona, and Phil Vincent have been a tremendous influence on my teaching. And I want to keep learning from the best—those wonderful educators and my students.

I've adopted some personal practices that seem to make a huge difference in the mood and manageability of my classroom. I've described them here in the way that I use them—you may need to adapt them to your own particular style and the age of your students, etc. Every classroom and group of students are different. Some ideas I got from others and have tweaked them to fit my situation. I work hard all the time to make my room a true learning center where students want to be. If you see some ideas that you like or want to try, give them a good, honest effort. You don't have to wait until next year, next semester, or next week. Go ahead and give something new a try tomorrow or as soon as you prepare for it. It is never too soon to start winning and having fun at teaching!

## Handshake

### Models respect, integrity, trust, cooperation

This may be the slightest and easiest change you make to your daily routine, but it may also be the greatest. There is no trick. All I'm talking about is simply shaking the hands of all your students as they enter the classroom! In the half a second you took to shake that hand, you had a direct, meaningful, personal connection with that student. It's a chance to connect with every single student every day! Hal Urban calls it transferring positive energy at the door. Harry Wong says it's the only way to start every class. A simple handshake makes a personal connection between you and each student, fosters a respect and integrity, and begins a relationship.

Think about what a handshake is—a greeting, a symbolic gesture of partnership and togetherness. Look at it throughout history. The handshake has ended wars, obtained great wealth, created powerful alliances. The refusal of a handshake has led to devastation, death, and demise!

Handshakes are unique and often personalized. I remember my dad telling me when I was a small child about the importance of a firm handshake, and what it said about your character.

What if you or your students aren't comfortable with a handshake? Then you might want to substitute it with a high-five, or even a touch on the shoulder. If you have any students who clearly doesn't want to be touched, then don't touch them. Respect their space and comfort level. They will usually become more receptive over time.

If you don't get 'em at the door, walk up and down the aisles when you enter the room to shake the hands of the kids you missed. They will deeply appreciate the time and connection. Shaking the hands of your students daily may take up a whole minute, but the benefits of it could last forever!

You can even make it into a lesson if you want. Last year my economics class and I spent half of a period one day talking about the value of a good handshake in the business world, on job interviews, meeting a date's father, and what a positive human resource it can be. We practiced it regularly the rest of the year.

## Saying "Thank you"

**Models respect, appreciation, caring, responsibility**

Is there any more important, positive two-word phrases in the world? We probably all teach our own children at home to say "thank you" any time we receive something, just as you were probably reminded hundreds of times as a child: "What do you say?" Most of us probably model saying "thank you" at home for our children, but how often do we model it at school for our students? Once again, something so simple can make all the difference in the world in your classroom climate and in your relationship with your students!

I discovered the value of "thank you" in the classroom several years ago from a student named Stefanie. Stefanie was a bright young woman in my U.S. History class. An underachiever from a single-parent home, whose mom was an airline stewardess, Stefanie was home alone quite a bit. A tough situation for any teenager! Though she was basically a good girl, she had questionable friends, by parent and counselor standards, and would definitely be considered "at-risk." She was tough, a loner, and quite sarcastic to protect her fragile ego. I loved her!

On an interim report midway through the second quarter, I marked Stefanie down for a B+, and in the comment section wrote "Thank you" with a smiley face next to it. At the end of class, after I handed out the interims, Stefanie came up to me as I was sitting at my desk straightening up. In a strong tone, she abruptly asked "What's this?" I replied, "What's what?" She pointed to and said, "The thank you." I told her I had written it because I knew she was working hard, completing all her assignments in five other classes, working a job after school, taking care of her household all by herself, and still doing well in my class. I told her I appreciated what she was going through and accomplishing—that's what I meant by the "thank you." Her face broke into a beautiful smile and a look of pride, mixed with relief, came across her face. She said that hardly anyone ever thanked her for anything, and certainly never a teacher. I thought she was going to cry. Heck, I thought I might cry. Ever since that day, Stefanie and I have had a close relationship and certain bond. "Thank you" had made all the difference in the world!

I never thought of thanks as an educational tool, but after I saw the difference it made to Stefanie, I use it every chance I get. Over the years, hundreds of students have made comments to me similar to Stefanie's. They *love* feeling appreciated. Students appreciate when we realize all the things they do and how they, too, are burdened with many commitments. That feeling changes their whole outlook about the class and about me as their teacher.

Saying "thank you" to our students builds a mutual respect, a sense of caring and empathy, and that appreciation is one more solid thing to build a relationship upon.

## Coach's Corner

### Develops respect, trustworthiness, caring

My coach's corner has always been something that I thought was important for me to do as a teacher. It's simply a corner of my room, often where I have my desk, where I put up things on the wall, or shelves that are a reflection of me as an individual. That's where I have pictures of my family, team pictures, my children's artwork, Michael Jordan pictures, Redskin stuff, awards and certificates…you get the idea. This is a part of my room where my students can learn more about me. They can see me as a real person who likes to play, laugh, and have fun just like they do. It personalizes me, so I'm not just another adult in the front of the room telling them what to do. They get to see me as a father, husband, friend, fan, and professional. My kids have always loved to ask me about the things in the coach's corner. It has led to some great discussions about more than the text book, as well as some good basketball games with my kids after school!

Please keep in mind the stereotype that students have about all teachers before they even walk in our rooms. They have this image that we're non-social beings that live and breathe their subject, grading papers twenty-four hours a day. They come in with a preconceived negative impression of us, before we even open our mouths. Sadly, some teachers live down to that negative expectation, feeling that they have to be hard on the kids the first few weeks to gain control. I don't agree with that philosophy. I think the student-teacher relationship built on mutual respect, trust, and caring will go much further than one based on fear and intimidation. First impressions go a long way—especially with kids.

The first time I realized teachers were normal, semi-normal anyway, able to laugh and joke, was during my student teaching my senior year of college! I was amazed, and relieved, too. I decided then I would do something in my own classroom to let my students know who I really was. My coach's corner was it. It's also good for me. I enjoy looking at it, seeing many of the things important in my life. School takes up a lot of time— time I could be at home with my family. Having the coach's corner lets me have a little of my family with me all day long.

# The "Away Game"

**Models respect, trustworthiness, caring, empathy**

The "away game" is me going to see my students on their turf. The classroom is a teacher's turf, where we are comfortable and in charge. The away game means going to see our students where they work, play a sport, or participate in any extracurricular activity. When we're there, the student feels more comfortable, a little more in charge. When we take the time to go to a band performance or to a play our students are in, we make a powerful impression—they realize we are taking our time to go see them, and they're terrifically impressed. Make sure they know you are there. Tell them they did a great job. Now they know that you care about them as more than just a test score. You immediately improved that relationship, both in class and out. Possible behavior problems will often cease, simply because that student knows that you care about him or her in particular.

Many of my students in high school work. They love it when I stop by their place of employment. Then we have switched roles. Now I'm the one who doesn't know everything about the situation, and they get to "teach" me. I'll never forget going to eat at Shoney's one night with my family. A behaviorally challenging student I'll call "Gus" was our waiter. I didn't even realize he waited tables there, but we became his star guests. He worked hard to make sure we knew that he had mastered his job. Gus introduced his manager to us, talked about school and things he needed to do better. Here was a kid who was BEH and in perpetual trouble at school, now being the perfect employee. He was working hard, earning a decent wage, and knew what he was talking about. That encounter improved our relationship for the better. I had positive personal things I could ask him about, and he could always ask about my family, and when I was coming back to Shoney's. The power of the away game should never be underestimated.

## Physical Environment

### Develops determination

The physical environment of our classrooms is tremendously important in determining the climate, atmosphere, and mood of the class. When I say environment, I'm referring to the walls, bulletin boards, chalk boards, desks and sounds. This is an area where most elementary teachers do an outstanding job. Their many decorations are bright and fun. There is color. Research shows that a child's creativity and active thinking are increased when they are visually stimulated. Secondary teachers, high school more so than middle, need to do a better job imitating their elementary peers. I've heard many high school teachers say "That stuff is childish" or "This isn't elementary school."

They are right. The posters and bulletin boards in middle and high schools need to be geared towards the older students.

A former principal of mine, Earl Crotts, used to say he loved coming into my classroom because as soon as he walked in, he could tell what subjects I taught. There are historical front pages all over, a large U.S. flag, numerous pictures of historical figures, all to go along with motivational banners, character posters etc.... My personal theory always has been that I may not be exciting every day, and every topic may not light them on fire, but, by golly, they can always learn something by reading my walls. My students love just looking around and reading the headlines and quotes. They like the color, too. I remember in college being told not to put much up on the walls because it would distract the kids, especially those with learning differences and/or attention deficit. I also remember how boring my room looked that first year with only a couple things on each wall. Now it's often those exceptional students who are most turned on to the class by the walls and decor. It helps them focus, and if their attention does shift visually, it shifts to something educational, making it easier for me to get them back on task. I also keep in mind the importance of first impressions, and each day when kids walk into our classrooms they see the room first!

**Notes**—Along those same lines, I have found that the way we present information for them to take notes has a tremendous impact on students. Taking notes was never my favorite thing, nor my students', so I try to liven that up a bit as well. I give a lot of notes, usually using the overhead screen. I always write in blue or black, but make a point to underline major points in red, and star important dates, people, etc. in green or purple. I usually write my headings in strong balloon letters, with color. All through high school and college, I couldn't stand it when teachers gave notes I couldn't read because of their bad handwriting, so I make it a point to print neatly and large enough. My students appreciate it greatly.

When I'm showing notes to support my lecture, I usually only uncover a couple of lines at a time, and try to give them time to complete copying and reading what they just wrote, before I start talking. Sometimes kids will ask to let them copy the whole page so they can get done and get it over with, but that's counterproductive because when they get done copying they often shut down, not listening as well to your explanation and points of emphasis. Hundreds of students have told me they love the way I give notes because they can remember it better when we do notes in short clips, explaining and discussing each.

For the last four years I've been hanging my overhead screen across a corner in the front of the room, next to the chalk board. This location has been a great use of space and has allowed me to fully use all my chalkboard without having to cover anything up. It also allows me more room to give notes, use maps, pictures, or whatever. It's also something different than the standard location—front and center. Kids do like a change of pace.

The chalk board is also a great tool that too many of us do not fully utilize. Besides the things I write on the board, such as daily assignments and things due this week—which I'll explain later—the appearance of the board is surprisingly important to students. Is it clean or is it dusty from days or weeks of erasing? My board is washed every single day, so the writing is strong, bright, and easy to read. Like my overhead notes I try to use balloon or decorative block lettering for note headlines, and use a lot of color. Students say they love my board and notes, and that it makes it so easy for them to read and pay attention to what is written. I love to use bright-colored art chalk. The clean board and colored chalk do take more time on my part, but the payoff in appearance, atmosphere, and student work level is well worth it.

**Music**—I have found music to be an essential component of my classroom climate. I use music in two ways. First, I always have music playing as students enter the classroom. Usually, I play a classical or piano tape. This creates a relaxing atmosphere. The great majority of my kids always ask early in the year if I will play this or that radio station or their tapes if they bring them in, but I don't do it. You will rarely get twenty or thirty kids to all agree on one type of music. Plus, I'm trying to set a tone. Exposing them to classical music isn't bad either! Within weeks they love the music and always ask me to play it if they are doing vocabulary, or writing assignments. Music really does seem to soothe the "savage beast"—the kids always work quietly and productively.

A key benefit of playing music as the kids come into class, is that it sets my class apart. Before I ever say a word, my kids know there's something special and different about this class! They like it!

I also mix up the music too. Often on Fridays, I will play a mix of rock, pop, soul, oldies, rap, top forty. Music is great at setting the mood/tone of the class and it can be a great pick-me-up during a long spell of dreary days.

## Daily Assignment

### Develops responsibility

This technique I heard about from reading and listening to tapes by Harry Wong. It's been a tremendous technique for me, and one that everyone should use. The daily assignment is the action of giving your students a short assignment to work on at the beginning of class each day. It should be posted in the same place every day. My daily assignments are designed to take only five to ten minutes, and to introduce my students to that day's lesson. I have used this technique daily for the last six years and will for the next thirty!

Having a daily assignment for my kids encourages—actually demands—responsibility. Every day when they come in, my kids know they are to read their daily assignment first thing and get started. Never is there a question of "What are we supposed to do?" or "What are we going to talk about today?" They know. There is no guessing or any delay by confusion. They like this because there are no surprises, and they gain confidence because they can prepare themselves. I benefit because I get five to ten minutes to take care of those tasks at the start of each period—taking roll, writing admit slips, signing notes…. It also gives me time to walk around the class and give some individual time when needed.

My students do not come to me naturally programmed to carry out this daily responsibility. We have to practice it at the beginning of the school year. (And usually after winter and spring breaks as well!) The strongest testament I can give to the value of the daily assignment and the responsibility that it helps foster comes from my first period class last year. On one particular day I had an 8 a.m. meeting that morning on the other side of town. I'd made arrangements for a co-worker to cover my class. I ended up getting to school about 9:15. Classes began at 8:30. When I walked into class my students were working diligently and quietly. I looked around to thank co-worker for covering for me, but did not see him. I asked my kids where he had gone, and they said he or no other teacher had been to class yet! I was happily amazed. I asked them how they knew what to do and why they were so quiet. Their reply was simply that they always knew where the assignment was and what to do. They figured I or someone would be in soon. I was so pleased and proud I told them that they had earned an extra 100 points on their next pop quiz. They had shown responsibility, respect, self-discipline and integrity—all on their own. Our routine procedures and the daily assignment had helped make these high school juniors pro-active, independent and responsible learners.

## "Celebrate a Classmate"

### Develops respect, caring, motivation

This activity may just be the best thing I did with my classes all last year. I heard about it from Dr. Phil Vincent, who told me about this super activity done by a California teacher, Hal Urban. When I first heard this affirmation activity described, I thought sounded kind of "fluffy," and had my doubts, but I'm always willing to try new activities that might help my classroom. Well, "Celebrate a Classmate" went so well that as soon as I did it with my first class, I ran next door and told the teacher next to me about this wonderful activity she had to do with her class! This really was one of the best, if not THE best thing I did all last year.

Here is how I set it up as a daily assignment. I wrote up on the board that I wanted them to celebrate a classmate—they were to write something nice or something they appreciated or admired about someone in class. At first, the kids had questions. I told them to write something nice about somebody, but not necessarily their best friend in class. I gave a few examples to get their minds into this mode because most high school kids are not used to doing this type of thing. They had to put their names on their papers, but I promised that I would not identify any authors when I read the papers. My students thought deeply and wrote quietly.

As I started to look these over to myself, I was really pleased, but when I read them aloud the effects enlightened my life! The comments written down included, "Derik has a nice smile," "Ian is smart and funny," "Steven makes me laugh every day," "Courtney is always nice to every-one," and "Crystal is here today. I have missed her." You should have seen their bright eyes and smiles when they heard their names and what others thought of them! It made everyone feel great, appreciated and special. Crystal's reaction was the greatest. She'd been out sick for three or four days, and this happened to be her first day back. When I read "Crystal is here today. I have missed her," her eyes lit up like beacons and the most beautiful smile I've ever seen in a classroom came across her face. She and I both melted. The young man sitting behind Crystal, Tim, had written this celebration. They were classmates, but had never been close friends. When Tim saw Crystal's smile and eyes as she looked around the class to see who might have written this, a warm smile came across his face. As my kids were leaving class at the end of the period I stopped Crystal and asked her why she seem so surprised and delighted. She said that she did not think that anyone besides me even noticed when she was gone! Now she knew differently. My students learned many things that day, the big one being that they do matter to other folks and do make an impression on others.

Many people ask what happens to the kids who don't get written about—aren't their feelings hurt? That's possible, but the way I used this last year, I was able to avoid that. I did this about once every three or four weeks, and I told my kids to write about someone different each time. They were very sensitive to others in the class, and many went out of their way to write nice things about classmates who might not have been included yet. To also safeguard against hurt feelings, at the end of the semester I made sure that during the assignment I wrote a celebration about each individual in class and read these aloud.

Celebrate a Classmate is something that I will do for the rest of my career. The way it builds that sense of caring and family in the classroom is phenomenal.

# Grading THEIR OWN Tests and Quizzes

**Develops honesty, trust, responsibility, respect, achievement**

When I first heard about this technique, I immediately had the same thought, concern or doubt that you probably just had: "Won't they cheat?" I've since found out, that no they won't—in the five or six years I've been using this, I found one student cheating and suspected only two others. That's out of probably 900+ students in that time period. I believe if a child is going to cheat, he of she are going to cheat anyway. I also strongly believe in these words of Booker T. Washington: "Few things help an individual more than to place responsibility upon him and to let him know that you trust him."

The sound, academic merit to this practice is well documented. Every study ever done on academic feedback states that the sooner a student receives the feedback, the more useful it becomes. You can't get any feedback sooner than immediate feedback. That is what students get when they grade their own tests and quizzes. They get to grade their own work immediately or the next day at the latest! Students immediately get to see what mistakes they may have made, and see what the correct answers are and why. When I do this, I go over the questions and answers patiently, and allow all the time they need to answer any questions. I take time to explain questions that may have led to any problem. The students love learning from their mistakes and having those explained while the material is fresh in their mind. This part of the learning process helps greatly come time for the next test or quiz. The additional learning also carries over to the end-of-course test. Achievement is directly and positively affected. I also let, and often demand, my students retake work that is subpar. This practice helps here as well. What we have now is immediate feedback, increased and active learning, and even more important, "mastery learning." Achievement is up. Self-respect is up. Responsibility is increased.

There is also a benefit to the teacher. I have not always gotten papers back to students in a very timely fashion. I still don't always, but this practice has helped greatly. As a father, husband, and coach, I also have other responsibilities just as important as my students' papers. It has not always been possible for me to get papers back the next day or two. I'm happy if I get them back in the same week in many cases. How many of us have done this—take papers home to grade, but don't grade them because we're too tired, too busy, or too interested in a good show on television, then take them back to school thinking you might get to grade them the next day, but you don't...so you start the whole cycle over again, sometimes for days! I call it the "Grading Papers Two-Step." I used to be the master. Now with letting my kids grade some of their own tests and quizzes, I do a whole lot less two-steppin'. The kids are learning more and I'm doing less! You can't beat it.

Let me clarify how I use this. I do not do this every time. I do it when I can, depending upon the style of test or quiz. You can't do this with essays. I also do this after we've been in school for several weeks and I've established a positive atmosphere and relationship with the class. There is a degree of trust and respect to build upon. The first time or two that I did this my kids were in shock. They wanted to change writing utensils or papers, just to show me they were not cheating. I told them I trusted them and explained how it would be better for their learning. They couldn't believe that a teacher was trusting them to grade their own paper. This is where the Booker T. Washington comes in. Students love knowing that you trust them. My kids work to make sure they don't abuse that trust.

## Partner Tests

### Develops respect, responsibility, achievement

When I first used this technique about five years ago, it was one of the best examples I had ever seen of active, participatory learning. It still is. The partner test is also a great way for the high school teacher to incorporate cooperative learning. I learned it from a Clare Lemeres workshop and have used it and loved it ever since.

It's a normal test, but the student has a partner to discuss answers with. I have always given my partners one test and one answer sheet. Both students use the same answer sheet and get the same grade. I have had some students, very few, prefer not to have a partner, so I let them work alone. I've also had the situation where uneven numbers forced me to allow a group of three students to work together. They all work together and get the same grade.

I set up my first partner test like I would any other. We have a test review or study guide the day before the test. On test day everything runs as usual right up until I give the test out. Once my students are ready I surprise them by telling them to get with a partner! They will be startled. Once everyone has a partner, I have them spread out around the room, so they and their partners may talk quietly without disturbing other groups. I tell them how the test works—one answer sheet, one grade, whisper.... I tell them they are to discuss each answer with their partner and work together to come up with the best answer. They love the opportunity to work together—cooperative learning is very natural—and they strive to do their best.

All the ideas I've suggested work wonders in my classroom to inspire active learners and considerate classmates. Though some of them take a bit more of my time—like the careful writing out of notes I want them to copy—others have handed me back more time to enjoy the company and eager minds of the young people in my classes. We both like the variety and stimulation they bring to the curriculum, and it never fails to energize me when a student says, "It's easy and fun to learn in your class."

# The Little Classroom That Could...

**Deb Austin Brown**
Character Teacher/Trainer
St. Albans, West Virginia

In a small-town elementary school, nestled in the beautiful mountains of West Virginia, a kindergarten teacher meets her new class of students. It is an unusual group for this middle-income neighborhood. Ninety percent of the students are from broken homes, forty percent have never met their biological father, sixty percent live with their mother and her current boyfriend, fifty percent live with a parent who is unemployed, and seventy percent qualify for free or reduced lunch. Ten percent of these students have a parent who is in prison for a capital crime. The first weeks of school showed this veteran teacher that eighty percent of her students had another problem...their behavior!

I am that kindergarten teacher. And, fortunately for me and for my students, I am also a character teacher. The first month of school was the most difficult of my twenty-one-year teaching career. I knew that before I could begin teaching academics to my students, I had to give them the foundation for all learning—the character message. And that's where we began our journey.

> Our self-confidence is built in direct proportion
> to the strength and structure of our character.

I thought back to my own childhood to find what this class needed. Many of the great character lessons I learned came at the knee of a caring adult. My great-grandmother was a wonderful storyteller, who ended every childhood story with a memorable moral lesson. These long years later, I still recall the great moral lessons of my youth. These lessons gave me a moral rope to hang on to during the decision-times of childhood... and beyond. In my class I tried to replicate those lessons, challenging my students to get the character message from every story. I taught them that everyone of us is responsible for carving out our own character by the decisions we make and by the habits we develop. As we began saying in our class, "Get the character habit!"

Using the traits of good character as the focus for all that I did, I tried to help students set goals and establish good attitudes, habits and a work ethic that would contribute to the development of their true potential. I believe that there is goodness and greatness in every student. And I believe that a foundation of good habits and work ethic will transcend the classroom to every area of a child's life. What a wonderful thing it is when the child's good *work ethic* becomes his good *life ethic!*

## From Work Ethic to Life Ethic

Teaching for character translates academically. That is one powerful lesson that we all need to learn. As soon as I learned that lesson, I was off to making a wonderful difference with the students I would teach! Two of the best lessons for ensuring academic success are the lessons I learned about habits and work ethic.

Habits are powerful in defining our lives and charting our destiny. Harvard and Stanford research shows that between ninety and ninety-five percent of what we do each day is attributed to habit. Those powerful statistics show how innocently habits begin as spontaneous decisions in our lives...and grow to become like cables that chain us to our old behaviors. Many of us end up learning the powerful lesson on habits the hard way. So, the choice is ours. We can intentionally choose to develop good habits that will serve us well, or we can incidentally acquire bad habits that we will spend considerable time and effort trying to break. What will you choose for yourself and the students in your life?

Another focus for our character message was work ethic. Literature is a wonderful teacher! The story of *The Three Little Pigs* gave us a great lesson on the importance of doing a job well. *The Little Red Hen* showed how those who work hard enjoy the fruits of their labor. And *The Little Engine That Could* showcased the importance of confidence, determination and perseverance. "I'll try!" became the class motto, ensuring that students would develop the needed confidence and determination to get any job done. I began to use the moral lessons of great literature to weave the character message into the classroom fabric of all we did.

In the spring, while doing a unit of study on wind and storms, we were constructing a Venn Diagram on the constructive and destructive characteristics of wind. One of my students suddenly said, "Gee, that's just like character! There are good and bad habits that either make the pillars stronger or tear them down." I was stunned, but quickly grabbed the chart paper and began recording their wonderfully creative ideas. These students clearly understood that good habits build up character and bad habits tear it down. One even remarked, as we listed the bad habits on the chart, that he could hear the pillar of character cracking and starting to break! In response, when we displayed our new character charts in the classroom, we displayed the bad habits pillar with a crack in its foundation. It was a wonderful visual reminder for the classroom. I noticed the students referring to it often throughout the school year. In fact, whenever a student was seen breaking a rule, another classmate could be heard saying, "Oh, no! I think I hear the character pillar breaking again!"

## CONSTRUCTIVE HABITS

*Build Up Character*

Helping others
Staying on task
Telling the truth
Showing respect
Being fair
Being honest
Following rules
Being responsible
Showing kindness
Doing the right thing
Having a good work ethic

**DESTRUCTIVE HABITS**

*Tear Down Character*

Calling people names
Breaking rules
Being irresponsible
Hurting others
Being selfish
Getting even
Being lazy
Giving up
Telling lies
Not trying our best
Taking things that belong to others

# The Power and Promise of Educating for Character

Every day in my classroom, I saw the power and promise of educating for character. I saw my students undergo an incredible metamorphosis during the school year. By February of this particular school year, I knew that my students had not only learned the character message, but had chosen to live it. One unusual morning proved the point. I had been up most of the night working on a project. The power had gone off during the night, and I had slept through the alarm. When I woke up in a panic, I called my principal for classroom coverage until I arrived at school. I hurriedly jumped into the shower, dressed, and put my baseball cap over my wet hair before driving to school. I was more than twenty minutes late. I arrived in my classroom to find my students alone, with no adult supervision. There, before me, was the most beautiful sight! All my students were at their tables, quietly at work. They were drawing pictures and writing in their journals. Each and every student was on task. The classroom was so quiet that you could hear the proverbial pin drop! The homework basket was filled with last night's assignment; student bookbags and jackets were hung neatly on their hooks in the lockers. The lunch graph was completed and tallied—and had been taken to the office. The academic day had begun without me.

I dropped my briefcase in surprise. "What are you doing?" I asked. "We're doing our work," was the answer. Then I asked, "Why?" Donnovan piped up, "Why do you look so surprised? You taught us to have a good work ethic!" Jeff went on, "Remember? We're the kids of character. We don't do what's easy...we do what's right!"

I couldn't help but smile. Once in a while you will get a little glimpse into the power and impact of your teaching. Cherish each of those precious moments.

I sat down on the counter by the classroom sink, took my hairdryer out of my briefcase, and began drying my hair. As I did, I watched the miracle at work in my classroom—an entire class of kindergarten students living out the character message right before my very eyes!

Yes, the beginning-of-school percentages for this class were certainly stacked against them. But despite the odds, one hundred percent of my young students had learned, internalized, and had *chosen* to live out the character message! It's a day that I'll always remember...and cherish!

## The Power of One

Never underestimate the power of one caring adult in the life of a child. That caring and interest carries a child a long way in developing a life of character. One year with a teacher of character can act as a catalyst for change in the life of any student. Remember, in our soaring technological lives, the most important element in teaching is still the *human* element. And just as one caring teacher can influence the life of a child, so can one teacher—committed to the character message—influence the direction of a school. Sow good seeds, and be a patient gardener. It takes time, but the harvest will be bountiful!

> *"There is no stimulus like that which comes from the consciousness of knowing that others believe in us."*
> —Orison Swett Marden

The best story of the school year comes from one of my students I'll call Cody. Cody entered school in the fall excited about meeting new friends and learning new things. During the first week of school, Cody told me that he lived with his mom, her new boyfriend, and his two little brothers in the nearby trailer park. "I want for you to know that my real dad is in prison—for murder."

I looked at Cody in surprise. Cody went on to explain, "Dad and his friends were trying to steal some stereo equipment. Dad's job was to hold the gun. It was supposed to be empty, but his friends set him up. They put real bullets in the gun. My daddy didn't know. He didn't mean to kill anyone, but it did happen."

I was shocked by the reality of Cody's story, and the way he told it. This veteran teacher could see into Cody's heart and could feel his pain. My heart was wide open.

"The charges were reduced to manslaughter," continued Cody, "so dad won't have to stay in prison forever. But he will have to stay for a long, long time." Somehow I kept thinking that *a long, long time* would seem like forever to this young boy.

> *"When you break a pillar you hurt everyone."*
> — Cody, age 6

During the first months of school when I worked with Cody, I used his father as motivation for Cody to learn his alphabet letters and their sounds so he could learn to read and write and communicate with his father, who was so very far away.

In December, Cody came to school excited. "I get to go and visit my dad!" he announced. "When, Cody, when?" was the response from his caring classmates. "Over Christmas vacation!" was the awaited response. Cody was especially excited because this would be a *touching visit*. "We won't have to talk over the phone with the glass between us," Cody explained. "I'll really get to touch my daddy!"

When Christmas break was over and the students returned to school, I was waiting by the classroom door for Cody's return. As soon as he entered the room, Cody's smile began growing. "Well...how was it?" I asked. "How was your visit with your dad?"

"It was wonderful!" said Cody. "I got to go in this room with my dad. And I even got to sit on his lap! We played checkers, and we wrestled. And my dad even got to tickle me. Do you know how long it's been since my dad tickled me?"

Cody turned to me. "You know, Ms. Brown...on the way home in the car, I just kept thinking about my dad. I didn't say much to my mom on the way home. I just kept looking out of the car window...and thinking. And, I just kept thinking that if my dad had been in your class, that he never would have gone to prison. He would have learned about good character, and he would have made better decisions with his life."

My eyes were overflowing with tears. A little boy, Jeff, ran over to see why his teacher was crying. A very observant Donnovan explained, "There's nothing wrong with her, Jeff. It's just one of her *good* cries."

Yes, it was one of my good cries. In fact, it was one of my *best* cries! This young student had just constructed the bottom line on life—and had reinforced for me the importance and the power of the character message. There is excitement, magic, power and promise in educating for character...ah, great promise indeed!

## The Power of Words

> *"As one afflicted with feelings of inferiority and poor self-esteem as a youth, I am particularly sensitive to the importance of caring, love, encouragement, and praise from those whose lives touch mine. Encouragement and praise growing out of love and caring have the power to change a life, and that life may in turn change others."*

— Dr. Norman Vincent Peale

Norman Vincent Peale, John Dewey, William James, and Dale Carnegie have all taught us that the deepest need in human nature is the need to be noticed, appreciated, and affirmed. In our classrooms today we have the undiscovered Einsteins, Lincolns, Edisons, and Mother Teresas of tomorrow. It is our job to believe in our students until they can believe in themselves. By taking a child under your wing and showing sincere interest and caring, you can help chart their character growth in powerful ways! The words of Cavett Robert can serve as a wonderful reminder: "Three billion people on the face of the earth go to bed hungry every night. But four billion people go to bed hungry every night for a simple word of encouragement and recognition." Your words of encouragement and instruction can be a powerful tool in the character development of your students.

Years ago, a talented kindergarten teacher, Nancy, showed me this wonderful analogy about the power of words. It painted a vivid picture in my mind that I will always remember.

A child's self-concept is a fragile as a piece of paper.

When a parent fusses at breakfast, "Deb, you're always playing around with your cereal. You're making yourself late for school every day. Aren't you tired of being late for school? Just look at you! You haven't even brushed your hair yet! Hurry up! Can't you do anything right?"

**RIP!** A piece of the paper is torn from the child.

Later that day, the teacher joins in, "Deb, I've already explained the directions once. Don't you ever listen?"

**RIP!** Another piece of the child's self-concept is torn away.
Soon, the piece of paper is noticeably smaller in size.
As the confidence goes, so does her ability to meet with success.
The proverbial dog begins chasing its tail. It's definitely downhill
after that.

Think of your own life. The disappointments of life always fill us
with self-doubt. At times, we've all wondered if we'd ever reach any of
our goals. Think back...to a teacher who was there for you—to encourage
you and to offer support. He told you that you were a special person, with
special talents and abilities. He made you see the good in yourself—and
he made you want to build on the foundation of your character. Because
he believed in you, you were able to believe in yourself. And you went
on—to tackle more problems, to learn new things, to make better decisions, to gain new strides, to climb new mountains, to face the world and
all of its challenges, even to challenge the world a little yourself.

**Words can tear down...**
harsh, critical, pejorative, negative,
demeaning, cutting, degrading, shaming

**Words can build up...**
motivating, supportive, positive, encouraging,
inspiring, expecting, reassuring, understanding

Believing in someone carries great power! A favorite story drives
home the point. Picture it. The kitchen table and a four-year-old. A mom
has supplied art materials for her daughter. The little girl is at work—
drawing, scribbling, and writing. Mom is working alongside her in the
kitchen. The phone rings and mom has to leave the room. The little girl
runs out of paper. She knows better than to interrupt her mom who is still
on the phone. She sees a clean white wall. She climbs down from the
kitchen chair and continues with her masterpiece.

A little while later, her mom returns to the kitchen. "Oh, no!" She
sucks in her breath as she sees the crayon-covered wall. But she catches
herself, and she takes an important step back. She smiles. She says softly,
and lovingly, and with conviction..."Deb, I can tell that you are going to
be a wonderful writer." My mom goes on, "But don't write on the wall
again because your dad won't like having to paint the kitchen."

That was over forty years ago. But I remember it as if it were yesterday. It's a vivid memory—a powerful message of a positive first response

to a child. It's the power that stays with me as I write books, presentations… and celebrations, such as this one.

My friend, Mike Mitchell, said it well: "Words mean something." And words have the power to change a life and chart a destiny. Be careful, and choose your words wisely. The lives of your students may well depend on it! Are you an architect and builder of human potential…or are you part of the demolition crew?

## The Power of Wisdom

I was raised on wisdom, and I still remember the stories and lessons that were part of my own childhood. An important part of teaching for character comes from the many *incidental* teachable moments that come throughout the day. But *intentional* lessons are also taught through the use of stories, fables, fairy tales, folk tales, proverbs and real-life stories from the lives of my students. The moral wisdom of these stories is repeated at transitional times throughout the school day:

Actions speak louder than words.

Honesty is the best policy.

The best way to have a friend is to be a friend.

Say what you mean, and mean what you say.

Hard work never hurt anyone.

You can go a long way after you are tired.

Don't do what's easy, do what's right.

Don't try to be anyone else, just be yourself.

Our decisions define us.

Be a good-deed-doer.

Be in the right place at the right time doing the right thing.

Follow your heart.

We repeat these messages when we're changing classes, lining up for recess, washing our hands for lunch, and packing our bookbags at the end of the school day. These character-building moments take no time out of our daily schedules, yet are powerful in helping students internalize the character message. By repeating the wisdom five or six times each day, 180 days a school year—my young students commit the messages to memory. It gives them a *moral rope* to hang on to for the decision-times of their childhood and beyond—making character a way of life!

# The Power of Metaphors

Real-life character messages are all around us. Creating an awareness of these natural messages is one of the greatest gifts you can give your students. Students are naturally drawn to these messages and their powerful life lessons. I believe that there is an innate desire in each child to be drawn to the side of goodness. Each student needs structure, boundaries, direction and guidance. That important job belongs to both parent and teacher. And when the home and school join hands in the effort—the impact of character training becomes all-encompassing! That consistent *teaching* then becomes character *training*—the most powerful of all in affecting change in the life of any student.

Years ago, I met a man who would change my life. Dr. William Mitchell had written a book called *The Power of Positive Students*. A college-professor friend of mine had given me a copy of the book to read. Dr. Mitchell's ideas were so in tune with mine that I just had to write him a letter. I mailed it off to his office in Myrtle Beach, South Carolina—not knowing the impact that book and letter would later have on my life.

I received a warm and wonderful letter back, inviting me down for a visit. I'm sure that it was no coincidence that our family had a beach house just seven miles from Dr. Mitchell's office, in Garden City Beach. I couldn't wait for my next beach trip! On November 3, 1992, I made the trip. That meeting began a new mentorship and friendship that continues to sustain me. One of the many lessons that Dr. Mitchell taught me was the difference between *interest* and *commitment*. Are you really interested in teaching children the character message—or are you committed to it? It's a powerful question!

So when I am in the classroom trenches daily, it's a question I often ask myself. Becoming reflective about all I do with kids, I question every move I make. Am I really committed to the character initiative with my students—or is this just a casual interest? Are my character efforts with kids *incidental*—or are they *intentional?* Are they an *add-on*—or are they *built-ins?* It's definitely food for thought!

> *"Values are built-in, not add-ons."*
> —Ben and Jerry's *Double Dip*

With so many character messages naturally around us, it makes sense to pull lessons from nature and from life. The best character lessons are life lessons. Dr. Hal Urban's insightful book, *Life's Greatest Lessons*, is packed full of them! I've read it from cover to cover four times, and I still pick it up when I need direction, motivation and a renewed dose of enthusiasm for life. The wisdom gained from just living life is perhaps the most valuable wisdom of all. Why not share it with your kids?

Often in the classroom I notice students struggling with classwork. Many students have not acquired the perseverance skills required to stay on task and complete the work at hand. One day, in an effort to help them with their struggles, I relayed the story of the woodpecker. "How many times does the woodpecker peck at a tree?" I asked. "Ten times? A hundred times? A thousand times?" Of course, I was searching for the correct answer: "Until he gets the job done!"

So we made a poster for the classroom. Students got out their markers and began drawing personal posters with big red-headed woodpeckers carrying the character message, "Keep pecking away!" Each student had a poster to take home, and there was also one to keep on display in the classroom. It helped...a lot! A fourth grade student in my Character Class came to school one day to tell me that he was "mad" at the woodpecker. "He just won't leave me alone," he told me. Jeffrey went on to explain. "Last night I came in from playing outside and had an hour until bedtime. I took a bath and got all ready to watch my favorite television show. Just as it came on, I realized that I hadn't done my homework. Now, I *really* wanted to watch that show! After thinking about it, I made up my mind to watch the show and let my homework go. Maybe I could get up early to do it in the morning before I left for school."

"How did you feel about that decision, Jeff?" I asked. He answered me, "I just couldn't do it, Ms. Brown. I was watching my favorite show, and there was that poster of the woodpecker. I could just hear him peck-peck-pecking away. I finally turned off the television and finished my homework. I knew that I couldn't stop working on my homework until the job was done." Wow! What a great ending to this kid's story!

Real life character messages give the school a common language for building character. The character messages are all around us. I think that a visual reminder always helps young children. In fact, those visuals help me, too! Just tuning in to the needs and interests of my students was the first step. Creating the awareness of the natural messages in our environment was the second step. Application to the real lives of children was the next. And so, I went on the prowl for meaningful metaphors that could reinforce the character messages I wanted my students to learn. I came up with lots! Sharing these with you may help you with your own search.

**Real-Life Character Messages**
- *Lightbulb:* Think about good character!
- *Exclamation Mark:* Get excited about doing the right thing!
- *Woodpecker:* Keep pecking away!
- *Picture Frame:* Picture it! Picture yourself as a kid of character!
- *Magic Wand:* There's no magic wand to acquiring good character. It takes work!
- *Building Block (A+B=C):* Attitude + Behavior = Character
- *Mirror:* Look for the best in others...and in yourself!
- *Star:* Get the character habit! It'll keep you in the company of stars!
- *Chalkboard and Eraser:* Each day is a clean slate!
- *Toolbox:* Stock your toolbox! (Stock it with good habits!)
- *Ruler and Yardstick:* Measure up! (Measure up to your potential!)
- *Doorknob:* <u>Run</u> through open doors (of opportunity)!
- *Pencil:* Write down your goals!
- *Basketball Net:* Keep your eye on the goal!
- *Barbell:* Pump yourself up with good character! (Strength training)
- *Target:* Target practice helps!
- *Candle:* Let your character shine through!
- *Sunglasses:* Good character is so bright...you'll need shades!
- *Broom:* If we all sweep in front of our own doors, the whole school will be clean!

These character messages are wonderful ways to keep your students on task. They serve as gentle reminders of powerful character lessons. When woven into the fabric of a school, they give students and teachers a common language. Students have stopped me in the cafeteria line just to say that they are *stocking their toolbox* or *pumping themselves up with good character*. We're speaking the same language. I know just what they mean, and it's a real joy to hear the kids speaking the language of good character with one another!

# The Power of Feeling

When young students first enter your classroom, they need motivation for learning and living the character message. Often that inspiration comes in the form of extrinsic motivation. Children thrive on recognition and praise for their good efforts and deeds! Words of praise, smiles, hugs, pats on the back, and certificates of recognition are wonderful ways to start off the character effort. But even the youngest students need to learn that there is a feeling you will get in your heart that comes from doing the right thing. I always tell them about it so that they will know that it is the ultimate goal for learning and living the character message. I tell them that the special thing about *the feeling* is that no one can ever take it away from them. Even though they don't understand it, they can grasp the idea that it *will* come. By referring to it often, I build it up as something to look forward to!

I'll never forget that kindergarten year when it did happen. Cody and Donnovan returned from gym class to report, "Ms. Brown, you'll never believe what happened in gym class! Some kid in the other class broke two pillars of character!" "Tell me about it," I said. They went on to explain, "We were playing scoop ball with partners, and this kid in the other class took our ball. We told the teacher about it, and he lied to her. He said he didn't take it. So, he broke two pillars!"

"Two pillars?" I replied. "Yes, two pillars! He *stole* our ball, and then he *lied* about it!" they said. Cody and Donnovan went on to tell me how they felt about the incident. "We felt like kicking and hitting and doing karate-chops on that kid!" "What <u>did</u> you do?" I asked. "We thought about it, and then we decided to do the right thing. We just went and got another ball—and went back to playing the game."

"I'm very proud of you!" I told them. Cody excitedly commented, "The neat thing was…I got it!" "Got what?" I asked. "I got that feeling in my heart when I did the right thing!" Wow! It was time for another one of my *good* cries. All of Cody's classmates gathered around as he told them about it. As I watched, I just kept thinking…sometimes *children* are the very best teachers of all!

## The Power of Passing on the Message

The kindergarten kids and I had learned a great deal about the character message in our time together. We knew the next step was passing it along to other students in our school. We knew we shouldn't keep our character light hidden under a basket. We weren't sure how to get started, but we were looking for a way.

In a faculty meeting, our staff was planning a whole-school assembly as a celebration for good behavior and academic responsibility. There would be twenty-four students in our K-6 school who had lost the privilege of attending. I volunteered to take the detention duty. One of the teachers said, "Deb, why don't you consider teaching some of your character lessons to the kids in detention? Instead of them just doing busy-work, you could begin working with them—and give them the tools to work their way out of detention." Wow! What a great idea! The staff agreed. And out of that idea, *The Character Class* was born at Lakewood Elementary!

Over the 1997-1998 school year, the class began growing. A change was in order. We didn't want the kids to try to get into the class by breaking school rules. But the kids in The Character Class were talking about the class—and other kids were expressing interest in coming. They weren't sure what was going on in Room 111, but they wanted to check it out for themselves. The staff had to ask a serious question: Do we want the kids *to want* to come to the class?

I decided a new game plan was in order. I opted to give up my Thursday planning period so I could open up The Character Class to anyone who wanted to attend. Every other Thursday, I would go to the school intercom and make the announcement, "The Character Class will meet today in Ms. Brown's classroom from 1:00 until 1:30. Everyone is invited!" Little did I know what would happen...and how that simple announcement would change my life!

The class grew! At 1:00, the kids started pouring in. Kindergarten kids, third grade kids, fifth grade kids...in they marched. They sat at tables, in extra chairs, and on the floor. They sat, smiling and eager to learn. By winter, the class was bulging at the seams! I was alone in the classroom with 60 or more energetic students, and I loved every minute of it! I expanded the class so we could meet each Thursday, and by spring, we had over 100 students attending the class, sitting everywhere...even in the window sills! Had the fire marshal visited, something very serious would have happened to me. But I loved this class and didn't want to give it up. The kids were respectful, well behaved, and learning the character message. There was an incredible excitement in this room!

The staff suggested that I divide the class into two groups—primary and intermediate. I fought the suggestion because there was something so special about all of us being in there together. The principal and staff had noticed an increased rapport between older and younger students in the school. The younger kids were looking up to the older kids for advice and example. And the older students were rising to the challenge! The younger kids had learned that the older kids really liked them—and that they learned from them as well. The primary kids felt like they had an important contribution to make. Our school even saw better Buddy Projects going on than in previous years. We were really coming together as a school! There was an almost palpable, new sense of unity.

Out of desperation to keep my class together, I posted a note on the refrigerator door in the Teachers' Lounge: "Teachers, sign up here for a free planning period on Fridays. The Character Class is going on the road!" I would give up my Friday planning period and go into Lakewood classrooms to continue the class. It took about 48 hours for the list to be filled with takers. I had each Friday for the rest of the school year filled!

At first, I thought that the teachers would leave the classroom for a well-deserved break while I was teaching their class. Soon I noticed they were choosing to hang around. They would sit at their desk and grade papers or work on lesson plans. But they were listening! It was a wonderful way to model good character teaching. It also helped them to become more confident in trying a few new things themselves. It worked like magic! Before I knew it, we had gathered a team of interested teachers, all of whom wanted to make the character message a part of the life of our school. So, out of The Character Class for students, The Lakewood Character Team of teachers was born! It was one of my happiest moments!

By the end of the school year, The Character Class had reached 253 of Lakewood's 357 students. Not a bad first year! Many teachers worried that I was giving up too much because I had "given up" my Thursday and Friday planning periods. **Believe me, I gave up nothing!** I got back *much more* than I gave! In addition to learning from the kids, I got that wonderful feeling in my heart that comes from doing the right thing. And, what I learned changed me forever.

Some assessment of The Character Class was now in order. After all, we needed to revisit the original intent of the class—to help students become more responsible learners. So, I did my homework. After collecting the data, the results were tallied and shared with the staff and parents. Take a look for yourself at what we discovered.

## The Character Class

- 68.7% of students reported an improvement in behavior and responsibility.
- 66.5% of students reported academic improvement: more completed classwork and homework assignments, better weekly test scores, and better report card grades.

Parents were commenting about better behavior and responsibility shown at home. A favorite comment came from a parent who was wondering how I got her son to put his dirty clothes in the hamper, rather than leaving them as usual on the floor and under his bed. It was heart-warming for me to see the message learned and lived...everywhere!

## The Power of Moving On

During the spring of this wonderful school year, I learned that I had lost my teaching position at Lakewood for the coming school year. I was bro-kenhearted. It was hard to hide my feelings from the students. Everyone was talking about it. Lakewood had never lost a teacher due to staffing cuts in the thirty-five years the school had been open. Finally the day came when the kids in The Character Class asked me about it. They were very upset. "Who will teach The Character Class next year?" they asked. I had to say that I didn't know, but that I wanted it to continue. I had to prepare them in case no staff member took it on. So I had to ask them, "If no teacher steps up to the plate next year, how can we be sure that the character message will live on at Lakewood?" One hundred and ten stu-dents looked at one another. I'll never forget the look on their faces. And then, a fourth-grade student named Sarah gave us the hope we were looking for. "*We* will do it!" was the awaited response. It was what my melancholy heart was waiting to hear. "Yes, you can help each other con-tinue learning and living the message!" I told them. "*You* can make sure that the character message never dies."

One fifth-grade student went on, "Ms. Brown, will you promise us one thing?" I was almost afraid to answer. I really wasn't in a position to promise these kids anything for next year. "What is it, Andrew?" I asked. "Will you promise us that wherever you are next year—that you will teach The Character Class? If we can't have it, at least some kids will get to." Wow! You can guess what happened next...another *good* cry!

> "Will you promise us that wherever you go next year—that you will teach The Character Class? If we can't have it, at least some kids will get to."
>
> *—Andrew, age 10*

The school year ended. With a heavy heart, I packed up twenty-one years of teaching—and moved it all home. I drove out of the parking lot crying. As I looked into my rearview mirror, I got a last glance at the school marquee. It said simply, "Have a safe and fun summer. Character counts!" I felt a deep sense of pride that I'd left my legacy at Lakewood.

That sign is still standing on the street corner in my neighborhood, proclaiming the message. Character *does* count in this community. But, as you and I know...it counts in *every* community!

I'm happy to say that four weeks into the summer, I found a job in a hometown school teaching sixth grade. After meeting my new group of students, I knew it was no coincidence that I had lost my job and was forced to move on. These kids need the character message, too—and I am proud to be the messenger! It's time now for me to fulfill my promise to the kids in the Lakewood Character Class. It's time for me to teach the character class to my *new* students. And guess who's going to help me in the effort? My Lakewood students! We're teaming up on a new project where kids from both schools will work together. The Lakewood Character Class will visit The Weimer Character Class and help them with their efforts. After all, I think I just read somewhere that, in schools, sometimes *students* are the best teachers!

## The Power of the Journey

So, *you're* interested in taking your own students on the character journey? This book has given you a map of the different roads some of us have taken. Dr. Vincent has provided the road map, and the contributing authors have given you their best travel tips. Mine are simply this: Tune in to kids, create an awareness, and look for life's natural wisdom to create meaningful lessons in character for your kids. Cultivating the *character climate* is the most important step! When you love your students enough to weave the character message into all that you do, you are well on your way. By rolling up your shirt sleeves and trying things yourself, you will learn what you need to do for the kids in your life. Each year will be different. Remember to be on the lookout for the road signs along the way. The seed of an idea to teach character lessons during detention time grew to become a vastly popular character class in our school. And out of that class grew our staff's commitment to form a character team. In your own journey with kids, plant plenty of seeds along the way. Be a patient gardener.

There are times when you will feel frustrated and overwhelmed. I understand. I've been there. Remember that, for ten years, my classroom was an island of character education within my school. We were the only class intentionally learning the character message. And as you have read, we became *the little classroom that could!* We spread the message! With lots of hard work on the part of students and teachers, we became the little school that grew...in character! It can happen for you, too! The fact that you are reading this book means you have already begun your travels. There is a wonderful and exciting road ahead. I wish you and your students a successful journey!

**You'll learn more about a road by traveling it than by consulting all the maps in the world.**